Praise for *The*

"A unique and wonderful book, br_____ ____ ___ ___ ____ __ ___ _ills that arise from a lifetime in herbal_ ___ ____ ___, competent, and relevant herbalism guided by the application of insights that flow from astrology. Understanding that herbalism is harnessing ecology for human health, Jane Hawley Stevens has taken this insight much further by showing how the cosmic ecology of astrology can augment all aspects of herbalism, from gardening to medicine making to healing. This book is a major contribution to herbalism's role not only in the alleviation of suffering but the transformation of human consciousness. Thank you, Jane!"

— **David Hoffmann**, RH (AHG), fellow, National Institute of Medical Herbalists; principal scientist, Traditional Medicinals

"*Celestial Gardening* unlocks ancient truths about planting—and living—in lunar harmony. Prepare to cultivate your garden as well as your soul: Herbalist Jane Hawley Stevens guides readers in contemplative discovery of the organic connections among plants and creatures, the moon's cycles, and the rhythms of our shared Earth."

— **Carol Connare**, editor, *The Old Farmer's Almanac*

"In this easy-to-understand guidebook, Jane Hawley Stevens demystifies the moon and stars in relationship with nature and explains how you can use their powerful cycles to make your garden the most beautiful, bountiful, and happiest it can be."

— **Maria Rodale**, author of *Love, Nature, Magic*

"In *The Celestial Garden*, Jane Hawley Stevens perfectly blends common-sense gardening with empirical observation of cycles. Jane illuminates early wisdom in the plant–human relationship, and her writing style invites one to embrace the beautiful relationship between the sky, the earth, and their joint cornucopia."

— **William Morris**, PhD, DAOM, author of *Cycles in Medical Astrology*

"Tuning in to ancient knowledge is like a living meditation. You let go of your ego and surrender to the higher energy, where all is connected. Jane Hawley Stevens helps us remember to dial down technology and listen to the subtle, cosmic rhythms that support all of life. *The Celestial Garden* is a luminous gem of a book and a must-read for all gardeners and plant lovers."

— **Pat Crocker**, culinary herbalist and award-winning author of *The Herbalist's Kitchen*

"Who has been growing gardens of herbs and vegetables for over thirty years and is now giving you directions? Jane Hawley Stevens, in this wonderful book, provides experience, techniques, traditions, and nature-wisdom, along with her extensive herbal knowledge."

— **Matthew Wood**, MS (Herbal Medicine), founder, Matthew Wood
Institute of Herbalism; author of *The Earthwise Herbal Repertory*

"A gift to all gardeners! In this pragmatic, clear, and comprehensive book, Jane leads us into the garden of the divine with her easy-to-apply guidelines for living and gardening in harmony with the moon and star influences."

— **Atina Diffley**, award-winning author of *Turn Here Sweet Corn*

"I have visited Jane's magnificent farm, and her chakra garden is one of the most beautiful and magical gardens I have ever experienced. *The Celestial Garden* is a treasure trove of her lifelong experience with plants and stewardship of the land, and also the wisdom born of her deep connection with the Earth. This book is wise, delightful, thoughtful, and inspirational, while being firmly grounded in the practical work of raising herbs, food, family, and community. Jane's clear explanation of the movement of celestial bodies through the cosmos has given me new appreciation for how the moon exerts its influence. Her practical, step-by-step instructions and lists of gardening activities to engage in during various moon phases are beyond valuable. I also appreciate her insights into the planetary influences on gardeners and herbalists!"

— **Betzy Bancroft**, cofounder and core faculty,
Vermont Center for Integrative Herbalism

"Ah, to go back in time and be a young land steward thinking about birthing gardens and planting trees to reach for the stars! *The Celestial Garden* would have been my companion each morning over a steaming cup or each evening setting intentions for the following day. To know the connection to each cycle of the moon, and which planet close above, for planting seeds of varying types into which soil to enhance plant growth and the harvest and offer the best potential outcome for vibrant wonderfulness is, well, very cool. Jane adds a sprinkling of lovely family stories that warm the heart. This family of farmers and workers is a positive reflection of balanced Earth and celestial energies."

— **Margi Flint**, founder, Earthsong Herbals;
author of *The Practicing Herbalist*

THE
CELESTIAL
GARDEN

Growing Herbs, Vegetables, and Flowers in Sync with the Moon and Zodiac

Jane Hawley Stevens

Foreword by **Rosemary Gladstar**

Chelsea Green Publishing
White River Junction, Vermont
London, UK

The information in this book is based on the author's years of experience and experimentation with herbs. However, the author is not a medical professional and does not offer this work as an attempt to treat, mitigate, or cure any disease or medical condition.

Project Manager: Natalie Wallace
Editor: Fern Marshall Bradley
Copy Editor: Angela Boyle
Proofreader: Nancy A. Crompton
Indexer: Shana Milkie
Designer: Melissa Jacobson

Printed in the United States of America.
First printing December 2023.
10 9 8 7 6 5 4 3 2 1   23 24 25 26 27

Our Commitment to Green Publishing
Chelsea Green sees publishing as a tool for cultural change and ecological stewardship. We strive to align our book manufacturing practices with our editorial mission and to reduce the impact of our business enterprise in the environment. We print our books using vegetable-based inks whenever possible. This book may cost slightly more because it was printed on paper from responsibly managed forests, and we hope you'll agree that it's worth it. *The Celestial Garden* was printed on paper supplied by Versa that is certified by the Forest Stewardship Council.®

Library of Congress Cataloging-in-Publication Data
Names: Stevens, Jane Hawley, 1956– author. | Gladstar, Rosemary, author of foreword.
Title: The celestial garden : growing herbs, vegetables, and flowers in sync with the moon
   and zodiac / Jane Hawley Stevens, foreword by Rosemary Gladstar.
Description: First edition. | White River Junction, Vermont : Chelsea Green Publishing, [2023] |
   Includes bibliographical references and index. |
Identifiers: LCCN 2023037159 | ISBN 9781645022138 (paperback) | ISBN 9781645022145 (ebook)
Subjects: LCSH: Astrology and gardening. | Planting time. | Plants—Effect of the moon on. |
   BISAC: BODY, MIND & SPIRIT / Gaia & Earth Energies
Classification: LCC BF1729.G35 S74 2023 | DDC 133.5/8635—dc23/eng/20230927
LC record available at https://lccn.loc.gov/2023037159

Chelsea Green Publishing
White River Junction, Vermont, USA
London, UK

www.chelseagreen.com

To my beloved David, who has traveled this horticultural path with me, creating our life's dream, and who makes our farm look like a botanical garden and a Frederick Law Olmsted park.

To Forrest, for giving me the wings to start an herb business with your birth, and inspiring the earache remedy that set my path on trusting Nature first as the supreme healer.

To Savanna, for suffering through your childhood skin condition until we could figure out a remedy for it, thus creating what became my best-selling product for decades!

To Sylvie, for your presence of peace and joy, not only coming from you, but from me when you daily solve my tech questions.

And to the source of all my food, medicines, and health— awe-inspiring and cyclic Nature. May my efforts of devoted love and gratitude be a ripple in the ocean of inspiration for others to become Earth stewards for generations to come.

Contents

Foreword

When I first left home to begin the adventure of living on my own, I remember the excitement of planting my first garden. I had grown up on a small dairy farm in Northern California, and my family always tended a large, abundant garden. While we kids harvested and did a little weeding upon request, it was Mom and Dad who planted, tilled, and worked that garden so that it produced enough to feed a family of seven, with plenty left over to share with others. My parents' garden was so lush and abundant because of the good soil, enriched by all the cow and chicken manure and compost they added over the years. Watching them, gardening looked so easy . . .

I could hardly wait to plant a garden of my own. It was the 1960s, and I was studying astrology, herbs, crystals, and everything else considered "new age" at the time (though most of this knowledge was actually ancient, "old age," that had been buried and forgotten). It seemed only natural that I would decide to follow the astrological gardening guidelines I read about in *The Old Farmer's Almanac*. Although I didn't really understand what I was doing, I followed the guidelines somewhat faithfully, trying to match my tasks with the ever-changing Moon. But truthfully, I found gardening by the Moon and planets rather complicated and hard to keep up with. My garden turned out far less productive than my parents' ever had, most likely because I'd forgotten completely about soil preparation (no compost manure in my small plot)—and I gave up on astrological gardening. Looking up at the Moon and smiling at her beautiful magnificence as she transited across the night sky, I went back to simply hoeing, weeding, and watering when I had the time or felt the garden needed it.

Fast forward many years, and I had the good fortune to meet Jane Hawley Stevens at an herbal symposium. Jane sparkles with energy and glows with an inner wisdom. One listens when this woman speaks, and she speaks often and enthusiastically about herbs, gardens, planetary influences, and what she refers to as "celestial gardening." For over thirty-five years, Jane has taught others how to garden with the planetary influences as her guide. Her beautiful gardens and fields of herbs and flowers stretching for acres across the landscape of her lovely farmstead in northern Wisconsin are a testament not only to her gardening skills but also her understanding of the forces of nature, including the influence of the planets.

Celestial gardening as Jane explains it isn't so much a matter of doing specific chores under a certain Moon phase as it is "*a tangible practice that can help us engage in the larger energy that supports life.*" Jane approaches gardening in the same manner she approaches life, with complete respect and regard for the influences that nature, including the heavenly bodies, has on our daily lives. She uses nature as a guide to living life in harmony rather than discord. And this is the essence of what she shares with others.

Lucky for me (and everyone else), Jane was in the process of writing *The Celestial Garden* when we met. When she asked if I would be willing to write the foreword for the book, I hesitated only a moment before saying "Yes!" Because although I hadn't pursued astrological gardening in an intentional way over the years, I had come to understand the huge influence of the Moon and other planetary influences on plant growth and my gardens. And I knew there was so much more for me to learn. I was just waiting for the right teacher, and who better to learn it from than this amazing individual who had such a deep understanding and years of experience gardening in harmony with the celestial influences!

The Celestial Garden led the way for me, and it will for you as well, to a deeper, broader understanding of astrological gardening. You'll discover that celestial gardening isn't so much about following specific rules for when to plant and not plant, or harvest or weed, but rather, it's about cultivating a deeper understanding of the ebb and flow of life, and the effects that the Moon, Sun, and planets have on us as well as the seeds under the ground and the young sprouts as they emerge. It's about working together in harmony with nature so that we are flowing with, rather than pushing or shoving against, the elements. Or in Jane's words, "*practicing celestial gardening guides you to the open doors, so you don't waste time bumping into closed ones.*"

In the pages of this book, Jane covers everything one needs to know about utilizing the energies of the "superpowers"—the planetary and elemental forces of our solar system—and she makes this knowledge readily accessible and easy to put into practice. She guides us to see the big picture and then apply it to the everyday tasks inherent in gardening. We learn about when to start our seeds, how to propagate, how to plan and plant a garden, best times to water, weed, and harvest—and to do so when the planetary influences are at their best. Practicing the art of celestial gardening not only makes gardening more enjoyable and your gardens more abundant, but life in general becomes more joyful when we work with the elemental forces all around us. As Jane says, "Celestial gardening is an adventure . . . no matter how much you already know, there is always more to discover."

While *The Celestial Garden* is ultimately about gardening in sync with the Moon, Sun, and other planetary influences, it is also a book of wisdom. So much thoughtful insight and practical advice is contained in these pages. You may find yourself like me, reading *The Celestial Garden* not only for its helpful gardening tips, but also for its wise counsel about living a life more in harmony with nature.

Rosemary Gladstar,
herbalist and author, from her home
on Misty Bay, Vermont

Timing Is Everything

My meditation teacher, Ley Vaz Guimaraes, once told me that when we are "communicating with plants," it is really our intuition in action. This makes sense to me. It is a form of connecting to the life energy that connects us all. The Dao De Jing reminds us of the importance of living in harmony with the natural flow of the universe, rather than manipulating it. It is easy to believe that the life force that charges the cells in our bodies is the same force that charges all living cells, whether in people, animals, birds, fishes, plants, or microorganisms. As we deepen our awareness of that interconnection, we can refine our communication skills to discover more wonders of Nature.

Celestial gardening—which many gardeners call planting by the moon, or astrological gardening—is a tangible practice that can help us engage in the larger energy that supports life. When there is too much to accomplish in a day, practicing celestial gardening guides you to the open doors so you don't waste time bumping into closed ones. The idea of making gardening choices based on the phase of the Moon may seem a little irrational, but gardeners throughout time and across many cultures have found that gardening by the Moon is a practical tool that can improve our gardens and our daily lives. There is so much guidance from Nature that we simply overlook. The Sun and Moon are two of the most direct and accessible natural forces that we can consult to help us experience greater ease and joy in everything.

Celestial gardening has helped me notice and live in that truth. The more closely I weave my study of the rhythms and influences of the stars and planets into my organic practices and herbalism, the more I feel the importance of the web of life, both here on Earth and beyond. As I have experienced the support that comes from the energetic elements of Fire, Earth, Air, and Water here on this planet, it is an easy next step to look up with wonder and awe and see the same support coming from planetary influences. After over four decades of studying the support that comes from the plant world, it has been such an enlightening lesson to see support coming from above. We are in an infinite energetic support system from below and above! In fact, the more I discuss this with herbalists and others who live and breathe with Nature, the more we see this magical force supporting all our needs, by just being open to this wisdom.

Celestial gardening is an adventure, like discovering a path to a magnificent forest glade. You try the little-known path and see where it takes you, maintaining curiosity and wonder about what will happen next. You begin to tune into subtle clues and nuances around you. You start to experience at a deeper level how everything in Nature is connected. No matter how much you already know, there is more to discover. The opportunities for increased perception and expansion are infinite!

You also discover that in the garden, and in the rest of life, timing is everything. Have you ever started a project that came to fruition with ease, joy, and sweet results? Have you said something important but at the wrong time, and your wise words went unnoticed? Have you ever been grieving for a loved one who passed on and had the auspicious experience of their favorite bird suddenly landing nearby, offering comfort? Yes, timing is everything, and through tuning in to the Moon and planetary cycles, you can make your life—and your gardening—flow and grow more smoothly, with fewer obstacles. There is a great basis of wisdom in the adage, "There is a time to sow and a time to reap."

Another of my favorite sayings is, "Nature always wins." No matter what we do to overcome and control Nature, we eventually step back and observe that there is a bigger balancing act going on. The power of the four elements is impossible to miss: Fire destroying large swaths of land, Earth creating an increase in tremors and earthquakes, water rising and flooding many more regions than previously, and air so commonly polluted and compromised that air index warnings

The Shifting Baseline

Shifting baseline syndrome is "a gradual change in the accepted norms for the condition of the natural environment due to a lack of experience, memory and/or knowledge of its past condition."* It is frightening and sad when I think of environmental degradation in my lifetime, and no one seems to notice or care! When I was a teen, there was sufficient ozone layer that we put on suntan lotion to get a better tan—there was no sunscreen. Cancer was extremely rare. Fish were plentiful and came with no DNR warnings of having a toxic overload if you ate so many a week. Just one generation ago, the Baraboo River had several swimming spots that are now unfit because of toxic agriculture and silt runoff, ruining the sandy bottoms. People just accept these changes as normal, but for thousands of years fish were safe to eat and water was clean and pure to swim in and the sunny sky was not a threat.

Pay attention to that which sustains us!

---

* Masasha Soga and Kevin J. Gaston, "Shifting Baseline Syndrome: Causes, Consequences, and Implications," *Frontiers in Ecology and the Environment* 16, no. 4 (May 2018): 222–30, https://doi.org/10.1002/fee.1794.

are commonplace. It is time we pay attention and become the Earth stewards we are meant to be.

Although many people have been marketed out of their common sense by the insistent messaging from our consumer culture, some people are waking up, because what we are being fed is not nourishing our minds, bodies, or spirits. In fact, the increase in cancer rates alone is alarming enough that everyone should turn into activists, demanding our laws protect us rather than protecting the corporations. Culturally, we have been taught to believe in science and double-blind studies, never questioning who pays for these studies and if there is a hidden agenda for a particular outcome. Intuition, inner knowledge, instincts, feelings, folk wisdom passed from generation to generation, finding answers through meditation or spirituality—these often receive ridicule when put next to "scientific proof." A friend asked me once if I thought there was more to life than meets the eye. I had to laugh at her question, but then I answered from my heart. Of course, there is so much more. Before the invention of telescopes or microscopes, many astral bodies and the inside workings of cells were unseen and unknown. As we create instruments that cater to our senses to see farther into outer space and deeper into subatomic particles, more people accept these new discoveries as commonplace. But there is still more that our eyes cannot perceive—pure energy that I cannot show you with a scientific device, but that I know is there because I use it in my work and my life and have witnessed the beneficial results. I call it my white magic wand.

My Story of Perfect Timing

Sometimes, Nature presents you with perfect timing, being at the right place at the right time. I had that undeniable experience in my own life. It was Nature's perfect timing that led me to find my beautiful farm, where I have been growing herbs for the past thirty years. I had moved back to the Madison, Wisconsin, area after living for several years in Texas, where I never could connect to the land, although I loved the people. I found a place in Spring Green, the hometown of Frank Lloyd Wright, one hour from our state capital, Madison. It is a beautiful artsy community set on the Wisconsin River. However, I soon realized that my landlord was stalking me.

He would drive slowly past the house many times a day and would come inside when I was not present. At the time, my son Forrest was only five years old, and this situation made me very anxious. I decided I would have to move again, and this time I decided to seek out land of my own. I began looking for five acres or more within an hour's drive of Madison. For weeks I drove out to various communities and spoke with real estate agents. Even though I had a respectable down payment, real estate agents and bankers were not taking me and my plan to make a living as an herbalist very seriously. This was in 1992, and these businessmen made me feel like Peter Rabbit's mother, selling my baskets of lavender and chamomile. Returning from one of these ventures, in desperation I impulsively pulled into a real estate office that I knew nothing about. A wonderfully calm woman greeted me. I told her how urgent it was to find a home with land to grow herbs for my business. She said, "I think I have the place." The house had been rented for the past twenty years and the owner, who now lived in Illinois, had not visited since her husband passed away back in the 1970s.

Leaving the real estate office and driving up the bluff on Freedom Road was a transformative experience. Set in the largest intact block of southern upland deciduous forest in the Midwest, I felt like I was far away from any civilization, entering the realm of rare birds and abundant wildlife. Deep woods surrounded occasional farm fields, long protected from large-scale agriculture because they rest on top of an ancient quartzite mountain range and are too difficult to till. The surrounding land was gloriously lush and green.

No one was home that day, and we found a seriously neglected and abused but solid house set on 130 acres. The land was expansive and enchanting. When I travelled to Illinois and met the owner, Mary Stankovich, I found that she was an eccentric woman. Mary had never driven a car, and she had a soft spot for stray cats, housing up to one hundred strays at a time. I believe I was one of her stray cats. I offered her 61 percent of her asking price, and she accepted it! But her kindness extended beyond that. Because the local banks were stuck in the previous century and would not grant a loan to a single woman (even a woman with a down payment), Mary and I worked out a land contract, where I paid her directly for three years and built up collateral so I could obtain a proper bank loan. Although I will always thank Mary Stankovich for her generosity and kindness, I say this land I farm on is a gift from Gaia.

So much of that story is lucky timing. If I hadn't been harassed by my landlord, I would not have been so pressured to look for land at that time. If I had not impulsively visited that real estate office, I might never have known the neglected but beautiful farm existed. And if it had been any other owner, the deal almost certainly could not have happened in that miraculous way.

We have all had experiences that make us gasp, pause, and notice the web of life, both good and bad. "Timing is everything" always rings

Jane and David's certified-organic herb farm in the beautiful Baraboo Bluffs of Wisconsin. Photo by Dan Hagenow

true. And whether it's searching for a home or a friend, or designing and planting a garden, learning to tune into the ancient knowledge of celestial rhythms is like a living meditation. You must let go of your pace, your ego, and surrender to the higher power, where all is connected. You thought you were going to plant today? Think again! The phase of the Moon indicates that today is an auspicious weeding or harvest day. Look around, take note, and you will find out the stars are right. You will spot a row of carrots being devoured by weeds or some excellent strawberries ready to harvest that had gone unnoticed. In my thirty-five years of following astrological guidance in my gardening, I may have been begrudged and nudged out of my plans, but I have never found that the advice led me astray. Truly, there have been times when the rain clouds were rolling in, so I grabbed my seeds and hoe even though the planetary influences were wrong for sowing those seeds. After all, gardeners have practicality in their blood. I hope you find that, by following the celestial gardening guidelines I share in the pages of this book, you find joy with your gardening in a rhythmic cadence that leads you to finish all tasks with successful results.

Trusting Nature's Wisdom

Western culture embraces scientific "facts" implicitly (often without considering who paid for a research study and thus whom the researcher had to please). Learning through intuitive guidance, however, is not well respected. In a similar way, Westerners readily spend time outdoors enjoying the energy from the Sun, but mostly stay indoors at night and don't pay attention to messages from the Moon's energy. *New York Times*–contributing science editor Ferris Jabr writes, "The sun's immense power over Earth and its creatures is scientific fact; to endow the Moon with equal power is to embrace fairy tales and ghost stories."* Our culture prefers the overt yang qualities of life, discounting or eliminating the beautiful qualities of the yin: slower, quieter, and harmonious. The subtleties of life are what I am after. We have all had quiet circumstances when the truth was whispered into our psyche. Perhaps Nature has reserved some of the truths whispered by plants and planets for those who tune in with sensitivity, desiring guidance from Nature. And as you will learn in this book, the Full Moon would be a great time for that pursuit.

Nature gives us everything we need to sustain us, and more: Air, Earth, Water, and Fire. Yet despite this beautiful cosmos, we let governments and corporations exploit these resources as if we are asleep, oblivious to the need for balance and respect for our beautiful planet. Imagine if we woke up tomorrow to find that all the grocery stores on Earth had closed. So many people would not know how to survive! It is incumbent on us all to learn this truth: food comes from soil, plants, water, and the magical creation of sugars and oxygen from photosynthesis.

Once many years ago, I picked some mullein flowers and warmed them in olive oil. I put some drops of the oil in my young son, Forrest's, ears and watched as his recurring ear infection abated. From this simple act, I became a devout appreciator of Nature as the source of beauty and wellness.

---

* Ferris Jabr, "The Lunar Sea," *Hakai Magazine*, June 13, 2017, https://hakaimagazine.com/features/lunar-sea.

Astrological Attunement

We have all been put in our place when we simply had to give up on a project because our efforts kept hitting roadblocks, and we have all had times when a project just flowed like water in a stream. These are the subtle influences you will discover by paying attention to the influences of the cosmic rhythm, or astrological attunement.

It can begin as simply as noticing how the energy of spring causes plants to pop up in the garden. On some spring days, we feel the force of new life as powerfully as if it were a Ram (Aries). As spring unfolds, the energy shifts to a more nurturing warmth and energy like a mother cow (Taurus, Bull). And so, the seasonal rhythm continues, month after month and year after year. At first the idea of relating astrological energies to our gardens and daily lives seems far-fetched. Truly, it is fetched from afar but also from near at hand, because it pertains to the energy that binds us all into one. Both the energy that keeps all planets in their orbits and the energy that fuels plant growth and decomposition are as one.

Our modern world is saturated with technology—providing instant answers to any question via Google—but also many distractions that prevent us from listening to the quiet wisdom within. My practice of celestial gardening has helped put me in sync with cosmic rhythms and observe how the subtle energies are helping to guide us all.

My evolution into celestial gardening was an organic one. As a young adult, I decided to study horticulture at the University of Wisconsin–Madison based on some of my earliest childhood memories of the feelings that arose as I recalled picking blueberries in the woods with my grandmother. I still can feel the sense of expansion, wonder, and peace that I experienced that day, when I was not much taller than those wild blueberry bushes. The deep impression left by that defining experience persuaded my heart that I must pursue a career that would allow me to work out of doors. I chose horticulture, and from there, herbs chose me.

After I received my bachelor's degree, my first job (it was the year 1981) included the assignment to design and plant an herb garden. Thus, I approached herbs first as landscape plants. After installing my first herb garden, I was surrounded by herbs. I quickly started

Jane in her garden studying the relationship between plants and planets with her dog, HouChi. (HouChi is the Chinese god of agriculture and harvest.)
Photo by Kelly Kendall Studios

accumulating my herb library and, becoming immersed in herbs, kept expanding my interactions with them. I began using them in cooking and for making crafts. Meanwhile, I launched into my own study of herbs through books and other publications. It was fun and rewarding to learn the culture and uses of these beautiful aromatic plants. Every night as I studied, I became more familiar with all the various forms and uses of herbs. Eventually, when I met an herb in a garden or in Nature, I would recognize it from having gazed at pictures night after night. It was like falling in love.

I left the workplace to start a family in 1987, and my newly built greenhouse was a place to grow potted herb plants to provide some income while raising my baby, Forrest. With Forrest settled in his swing or playpen, I planted flat after flat, until thousands of herbs filled the greenhouse. This was the era when the "certified organic" program set up by regional groups first emerged. The USDA program did not begin until 2002, making things more complicated, expensive, and geared for big business. Entrenched in the love of herbs, Nature, and meditation, and intrigued with what I was learning about gardening by the Moon phases, experimenting with organic practices was a logical next step. I jumped on board the organic movement in 1989 and have been there ever since.

Around that same time, I began reading *The Old Farmer's Almanac*. It was intriguing to study the pages that designated "Best Days" for various farm activities. Eventually I engaged this guide as one of my farm practices, which fit like a glove with organic farming philosophies.

I am a double Aries with Moon in Capricorn. It you don't know what that means, no worries—by the time you finish this book, you will understand why it means that starting new things comes naturally to me! And indeed, every spring I would plant new seeds and seedlings almost every day from March to mid-June. Then, I would look around and see weeds devouring my early plantings! It could have been cause for panic, but celestial gardening principles guided me to weed around my young herb plants for two to three days when the Moon was favorable for that activity, and then wait a few days, focusing on other tasks, until the next favorable period for weeding. Almost immediately, I began to feel the satisfaction that comes following Nature's rhythms. I was grateful for the way it offered structure to my work, and I could see that following the patterns suggested by planetary influences led to successful growing. Since then, I have practiced and experimented using this guidance with wonder, awe, and success for over thirty-five years.

About This Book

The Celestial Garden is intended to inspire you to engage in this infinite web of superpowers by learning about the many subtle ways that the Moon, the elements, and the signs of the zodiac can influence plants (and people). In the book's first two chapters, I describe the movement of the Moon around the Earth and through the path of the twelve constellations of the Zodiac and how I relate the Moon's cycle through the constellations to gardening activities. I also delve into the science that underlies celestial gardening—how the Moon subtly influences the movement of water in the soil and thus the growth of plants. After I explain the basic principles of gardening by the Moon, I also describe the method used by biodynamic gardener, researcher, and author Maria Thun and many biodynamic gardeners. In chapters 5 through 8, I focus on each of the Moon's phases, from New Moon to Last Quarter, providing lists of gardening activities suitable for each phase and sharing some of my best gardening techniques and knowledge. The four seasons are also important markers of the cycle of the year, and in chapter 9, I present some of my favorite seasonal recipes for herbal syrups and instructions for making an herbal wreath. Chapter 10 describes a very special educational garden I designed and planted that was inspired by the seven chakras—centers of spiritual energy in the body. A couple years ago, while studying the planets, I learned the planets corresponded with the chakras, so I layered that knowledge into the garden design. In chapter 11, I turn the focus from the garden to the gardener, looking at each astrological sign in turn and how the personality and key qualities of that sign might relate to a gardener's special gifts and possible garden-related professions and avocations. In the book's final pages, I offer some of my viewpoints—personal, political, and practical—based on decades spent learning from the plants and Nature.

I am offering the information in this book as a seasoned herbalist and horticulturist rather than an astrologer. The plants opened the doors for me to become a student of astrology. To call myself an astrologer would be like someone who has studied herbalism for only five years claiming to be an expert herbalist. (Insert laughter here.) Please see this book through that lens. I am thrilled and honored to be able to pursue a path blending these disciplines. My dedication to meditation since I was in my twenties and my love of stargazing helps me see the unified big picture. Join me in this adventure, discovering how to make gardening and life easier and more fulfilling—the possibilities are infinite!

Postscript: As I was writing this introduction, my butt began to ache from sitting too long. I realized that I had lettuce transplants ready for the garden. The timing according to the planets was perfect for transplanting: the First Quarter in a Water sign, perfect for leafy growth. After they were in the ground, dark clouds rolled in. A light shower began, although none was forecast. This helped settle in my beloved future salads (although I did water the new plants well, too).

CHAPTER 1

Why Plant by the Moon's Influence?

Whether we move instinctively to the lunar rhythm, or must choose to synchronize ourselves with free will, if we want a broader support for our activities, it makes sense to keep Luna in mind. She offers temporal windows for beginnings and endings, and for everything in between. She is the consummate teacher of process.

—DANA GERHARDT, *Mooncircles*

The Moon was the original calendar, and the Sun the original clock. The power and rhythm of these lights guided human activities for millennia. Other than in tropical zones, humans also adjust their activities according to the seasons, which provide an overt natural rhythm. Tuning in to this energy as a natural guide makes as much sense as setting an alarm for the morning to start your day.

Spring starts here on our farm with the maple sugar season, and then we move on to planting seeds and filling the greenhouse full of medicinal herb transplants, flowers, and vegetables. Before we know it, it is time to plant the production fields. Summer is very busy with farm production and educational events. As summer turns to fall, it is the main harvesttime for our crops of herbs. After the autumn frost, when the leaves have succumbed and stored all their medicine in the roots, the root crops are carefully dug, washed, chopped, and stored. Seasons

The colors and moods of the seasons in Wisconsin: the greenhouse of spring, the field of summer, the changing colors of autumn, and branches covered in the rime frost of winter.

are pronounced dramatically in Wisconsin, each one marked by bright and subtle colors, weather patterns, and activities.

Planning activities by the Moon's influence helps to organize a schedule: when to envision new beginnings, start new projects, expand, then wrap up old projects. Did you ever start cleaning your house and have everything flow quickly and smoothly? Other times you just get stuck on every object: "Should I keep it or throw it away?" From major events to the mundane, you can discover how the influences of these cycles affect all aspects of life.

I find it is insightful, rhythmic, and fun to connect my planting and other gardening practices to the planets, as guides. I sow seeds at the time of the New Moon and harvest at the Full Moon. Even when I don't find anything to pick on a harvest day, I still appreciate following this tempo for the organization it provides my gardening activities, and simply because I am following Nature's rhythm.

The Moon and Water

Before the widespread use of mechanical clocks, people relied upon the Sun and Moon for timekeeping. A fortnight meant either the light phase of the Moon or the dark phase of the Moon (two weeks each). Traditional cultures from around the globe use Moon phases as a guide for when to plant and when to harvest. For example, in France, there is a saying, "*bois tender en cours / bois dur en décours*," which means "soft wood when waxing / hard wood when waning." This means that if you want to build something with pliable wood, like cheese boxes, the wood should be harvested as the Moon is increasing, but strong, seasoned wood for framing a house or burning should be harvested as the Moon wanes.

The fact that the Moon influences water is the basis of celestial gardening. The Moon literally moves water. The tides are an outward sign that the Moon affects the rising and falling of water. If you live near the ocean, you can watch the Moon's effect on water in the tidal fluctuations, with higher tides during the Full Moon. When a Full Moon or New Moon occurs, the Earth is in line with the Sun and Moon, as shown in the illustration on page 17. Their combined gravity causes very high tides, known as *spring tides*. This influence is also active underground, where we cannot see it yet it still affects plant growth.

The Moon also affects the movement of water beneath the soil surface, even in the heartland, the land-locked Midwest. Just as the tides rise and fall, the water table below is lifted, moistening the soil surface and making the germination of seeds more successful. You can use the knowledge of this phenomenon to enhance your gardening outcomes.

When the Sun and Moon are at right angles to each other (during a waxing or waning Moon), the Sun in part cancels out the pull of gravity from the Moon, causing lower high tides and higher than average low tides, known as *neap tides*.

The Moon's path takes it through the twelve zodiac signs, and each month sees the influence of each element—Fire, Earth, Air, and Water—every two and a half to three days. This pattern creates a nice tempo for gardening chores, and the activities are more disciplined and efficient by choosing those activities that would benefit from the current influence. It seems like an obvious connection that human beings, who are 60 percent water, would be influenced by the Moon. The same is true for plants, which are 80 to 90 percent water. In celestial gardening we also take into account the subtle energetic forces of constellations and the distant planets of our solar system.

Looking down, even though I cannot see the diverse populations of microbes in my soil, I realize all the support they provide. Looking up, I feel the subtle pulls of the constellations guiding life on Earth.

The Influences of the Stars

For some, thinking in terms of astrological forces seems very unscientific, for those not considered very tethered to the Earth. But consider early astrologers who watched the sky night after night and year after year, gathering elders' wisdom with each passing generation. They noticed the shifts in prevailing energies throughout the months and seasons. The astrologers then gave names to the signs of the zodiac to reflect those energies. If you think in terms of *archetypal symbols* when you hear the names of the signs—such as Aries, Gemini, and Aquarius—the concepts become more approachable.

The astrologers noticed the spring arriving with a strong energy, upward like the force of a ram scampering up the mountain (Aries). Then came the warmth of Earth in summer, like a mother nurturing

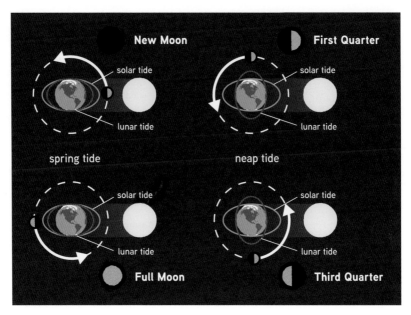

When the Sun, Moon, and Earth are in line with one another, the gravitational pulls of the Sun and Moon act on water, causing high tides in the ocean and lifting the water table in the soil. Illustration by Jerry Chapa

life (Taurus). The zodiacal names represent an energy observed. From this point of view, tuning in to cyclic energetic forces seems clever, like choosing an intelligent thought and action, while releasing a negative habit or backward act that does not fit your goal.

The zodiacal symbols also provide clues to their energy. For example, looking at the symbols pictured on page 18, notice that the symbol for Aries could be the ram's horns, or it could be a newly sprouted seedling, representing enthusiasm and beginnings. Taurus could be a bull's head. Like Ferdinand, the bull who did not want to fight but instead lay comfortably settled in a field of flowers. The curved horns might also represent sickles, which assist in collecting things (Taurus rules collecting). The two vertical lines in the symbol for Gemini represent the twins, connected by two crescents representing the higher and lower mind.

The history of planetary influences on gardening is ancient. In fact, Ancient Egyptian farmers left signs that they planted according to the Moon's phases. Systems for celestial gardening developed by

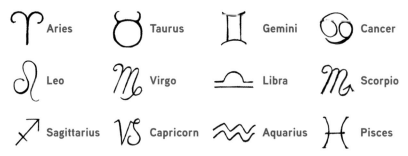

Look closely at these zodiac symbols and use your intuitive sense to connect with the energy they represent.

Indigenous people—from Europe to South America to many parts of the United States, including the Pacific Islands and Hawaii—exist to this day. In present-day gardening, the best-known application of the Moon's influence is in the system of biodynamic agriculture developed by Austrian scientist Rudolf Steiner in 1924. In chapter 2, I describe the Moon planting system developed by biodynamic gardener and researcher Maria Thun.

Both the zodiac and planetary motion are the basis for time measurement. The Earth travels around the Sun in a span of time now known to be 365.25 days. That's why our calendar is based on 365 days (with an extra day added every fourth year). Early astronomers in Persia and Babylonia determined through their observations that the Earth traveled around the Sun in 360 days and set their calendars to a 360-day year, which is one of the factors that led to development of the mathematical division of a circle into 360 degrees. The Moon travels around the Earth once every 28 days (27.3 days, to be precise). Because the Earth is also rotating on its axis, it appears to us that the Moon takes about 29.5 days to complete its orbit, a span of time almost equal to what we call to a "month." Think *Moonth*. One could approximate these numbers for easier calculations and determine that our 365-day calendar year is a compromise of the Earth's and Moon's yearly movement.

I appreciate the circular calendar. It is rhythmic and forgiving. There is a time to plan, then act; a time to plant, then weed. The square calendar seems less forgiving. As if when you mess things up, that is just the way it is, with no chance of fixing the damage done. That time has passed, and we move on, crushing the month gone by as its calendar page is tossed in the trash. With a circular calendar, time evolves and revolves: a time will come to clear up mistakes and be outward, or to clean the house or garden shed and be inward.

We know that all life on Earth responds to the Sun. The Moon is the closest planet to Earth (technically a satellite, but as you will see, it has the same effect as planets), and it makes sense that it has an influence on us watery beings as well. The lunar calendar closely matches the human biological cycle. The approximate 28 days in the Moon's cycle around the Earth is the same as an average menstrual cycle. We are part of the cosmic rhythm, and it takes less effort to go with this flow. We can tune in to each month's cyclic rhythm, complete with the influences and energetic nudges of each zodiac sign.

The planets also circuit around the Sun, each with its own rhythm. The planets travel on the ecliptic plane, which is the plane of the Earth's path around the Sun extended out into the celestial sphere. Most of the planets in our solar system travel within eight degrees of this cosmic ring. When I ponder this, I feel a deep sense of gratitude that we are set in a place surrounded by these beautiful twinkling lights for our enjoyment. Lights that we relied on in the past and still use for navigation. Perhaps we can once again integrate these heavenly rhythms into our personal journeys.

The zodiac constellations lie along this path as well and all of them are visible from both the Northern and Southern Hemispheres of Earth every month. As the Earth travels around the Sun, we perceive the Sun "moving" from one constellation to the next. The Sun appears to pass through the twelve constellations over the course of a year (thus, it changes sign about once a month). We also see the Moon against the backdrop of the constellations, and the position of the Moon relative to the constellations changes every two and a half to three days, cycling through all twelve constellations in about one month's time.

The premise of celestial gardening is to plant, transplant, and propagate under moist influences—Water and Earth signs—and to cultivate, harvest, and dehydrate for storage under dry influences—Air and Fire signs. (In chapter 3, I explain which signs fall into each of the four categories.)

Most people do not notice or care when the full Moon arrives each month. In our modern culture, roads and buildings are all brightly lit by LED lights, their glare dominating the darkness. This blots out our view of the night sky, separating us from our universe, but also having health implications. According to the National Library of Medicine at the US National Institute of Health, it has been reported in a meta-analysis that exposure to artificial light at night (ALAN) can cause sleep disorders, circadian phase disruption, and even breast cancer. Light intensity at night can suppress melatonin production, leading to difficulty in falling asleep or staying asleep, which causes negative effects on psychological, cardiovascular, and metabolic functions. Even bright lights in buildings during the day can cause these same negative effects.* A 2022 research study published by Sleep Foundation concluded that the popular belief that the Full Moon affects the quality of sleep is true. I can affirm that! My sleep is nearly always interrupted two days before the Full Moon but improves after.

Other reports verify that women tend to ovulate during the dark phase of the Moon. And in a two-year study, most accidents were reported two days before the Full Moon. The incidence of crimes is much higher on full Moon days, especially homicide and aggravated assaults.

The Moon's subtle influences are like the creatures that live out their lives deep in the ocean—not seen but very dynamic, rhythmic, and complete. In fact, corals release eggs at the Full Moon, but mysteriously, they do so only once a year. Truth is stranger than fiction and is mysteriously captivating. I find that studying Nature leaves no time for reading fiction, because the closer I look, the more I realize I don't know.

Why Tune In to the Moon's Phases?

Tuning in to Nature's cycles puts you in the rhythm of "what is"—for example, accepting that it's natural for humans to sleep at night and be awake during the day. Living in the northern climate of Wisconsin, the seasons demand that I move within Nature's cycle: plan in winter, plant in spring, grow in summer, and preserve food in autumn.

---

* Jay Summer, "Do Moon Phases Affect Your Sleep?," Sleep Foundation, January 6, 2023, https://www.sleepfoundation.org/how-sleep-works /do-moon-phases-affect-sleep.

Tuning In to the Moon's Energy

As we tune in to anything, eventually our sensitivity to the stimulus increases, like learning to play an instrument. We can feel the subtle changes of life that ebb and flow, beginnings, ending, sunrises, sunsets, like how a musician can hear one note out of place. We may notice that our sensitivities bring growth that affects our lives but also that our subsequent positive thoughts and actions can improve our family, community, and society. Think about the energy of Aries—enthusiastic, initiating, pioneering—and how that might inspire you to be brave and act, where you otherwise might not take the risk without the inspiration of that Fire sign. Save communication for a period with an Air sign, to support the conversation. (More on this in chapter 3.)

Following the Moon's cycle is another way of tuning in to Nature's cycle. Moon cycles can guide us on when to use each tool in our life toolbox. For example, if building a shed, the New Moon guides us to begin with a "measuring tape" in drawing up a plan. The First Quarter suggests we bring out a "hammer and nails" to build the shed from our plan. In the Full Moon, we pull our "paintbrush" out and complete the shed with a beautiful paint job. The Last Quarter encourages us to relax and enjoy our shed, and then dream up the next project to build something new again. This puts us in a natural rhythm with the energy that is flowing through life.

Here are some other benefits of gardening and living by the Moon:

It fine-tunes your gardening practices. Gardening requires a variety of activities, including soil preparation, sowing seeds, transplanting, mulching, weeding, watering, harvesting, and preserving the harvest. Some of these actions respond best to moist situations and others give best results under dry conditions. Both the Moon's phase and the corresponding planetary influences create nuances that can benefit or deter desired outcomes.

It offers a rhythm to your gardening. Are you like me and prefer planting to weeding? Following the Moon signs and phases guides you to keep gardening activities in balance. The weeding gets done, and you don't overplant so much that you can't keep up.

It encourages efficiency. You will find it easier to map out your movements and actions to be more economical—go with the flow.

It brings out the best. You can tap into the best qualities each sign has to offer and magnify those qualities in your life through meditation, focus, and action.

It increases your awareness and knowledge. Intentional awareness of what influences are taking place in the astral puts you in oneness with all that is and increases your observation skills. Pausing to observe life and tuning in to the senses are great ways to gain knowledge, which can cause positive changes for the world.

It leads to joy. Following Earth's rhythm creates sensitivity to the Laws of Nature and makes it easier to find and express gratitude, love, tolerance, and forgiveness. This will create more joy and ease in life.

The effort a gardener puts into planting seeds, improving soil, and maintaining each seedling as it expands into its fully blooming form can be immense. Working around heavy rains, hail, wind, and drought challenges the gardener, too—and increases the value of your harvest! A wonderful sense of exchange with the great creation can be experienced with this awareness and cultivation of gratitude.

Growers all over the world have noticed the climate shifting, making this process much trickier than in previous generations. My friend and colleague Josef Brinkmann sources herbs from around the world for a prominent herbal tea company. He has commented that growers all over the world are saying the same thing: "There is no normal weather anymore." In fact, a new term has been coined: "The new abnormal." Once he was visiting herb farms in the Faiyum Oasis, west of the Nile, where the year's crop was harvested and laid out on sheets to dry. A black cloud came overhead and hailed on the entire year's work, causing flash flooding, and ruining the crop. The growers were beyond dismayed, never having experienced hail in their lives. They could not help but feel as if something of biblical proportions was taking place.

This event tells me that *now is the time more than ever* to tune into Nature's rhythm. Because growing carries additional risk, it makes even more sense to concur with the cosmic energy that is expanding, contracting, and shifting all the time. Now is the time to pay attention to how the planet, plants, and people fit together in this giant dance of energy. Would you tango to a waltz?

Timing for optimal potency and shelf life of your desired flavors or constituents can be fine-tuned by employing the effects of the planets. I have improved the quality and extended the length of time my sauerkraut stays secure by consulting the Moon phases and the zodiac influences. I used to be frustrated when a batch of sauerkraut would mold in a few months. Once I learned about fermenting with the Moon phases, I had much better luck preserving the kraut from year to year.

One year I planted carrots with precise timing according to the Moon phase—the Last Quarter in an Earth sign (Taurus, Virgo, Capricorn). Then came the harvest. I felt inspired in the First Quarter to get those carrots out of the ground. This was not favorable according to the Moon phase, but I figured they had grown well, and I had my situation in place to store them for the winter. One day the following year in early spring, I decided to sweep out that messy area, and I lifted the garage door to sweep the debris outside. The bucket of stored carrots was in the way, so I moved it outside while I was cleaning. Whatever interrupted me, I do not remember, but somehow the carrots were left outside after I finished and closed the garage. Sure enough, a deep freeze happened, and I lost the remaining carrots. That is how celestial gardening works—strange and mysterious things happening either favorably or unfavorably as you follow (or not) these natural laws. There are many stories like this one—as my husband David says, "complete head-scratchers." Several of my students have spoken of strange coincidences in planting, harvesting, cutting wood, and other activities that can be timed properly while dialing into celestial gardening through the years. A nonbelieving husband became a follower of celestial practices after having good experiences cutting wood according to the Moon phases and astrological signs, and strange things happening unfavorably when he made the choice to cut wood independent of the signs. I find it fascinating to observe Nature's nuances through this lens of mystery.

The rhythms play out like a symphony when you align to planetary guidance. Plant seeds as the energy turns from inward to outward, and watch your crops expand as the Moon moves to full. When energy culminates at the Full Moon in a later month, rejoice! Your crops are ready to harvest. In the Last Quarter, as the energy closes, rest, regroup, and dream up your next endeavor.

When you pause and ponder when the correct timing is, sometimes intuitive knowledge emerges. Becoming introspective, receptive to this ancient knowledge, you become quieter, your sense of wonder opens, and new information can be received. Observe and tune into Nature's rhythm with the desire to gain a piece of her infinite wisdom.

CHAPTER 2

The Moon's Cycle
and Influences

Astrology is a study and use of the forces of Nature as an aid
in obtaining the highest possible degree of success, as a tool
to be used along with other helpful advice and information.

—LOUISE RIOTTE, *Astrological Gardening*

When people talk about astrological signs, they are usually referring to the Sun signs. In classical astrology, your Sun sign is determined by the position of the Sun and the zodiac constellation behind it on the date, time, and place of your birth. That constellation imprints various characteristics on you, like a prism throwing a rainbow of specific colors around a room.

But you also have a Moon sign. It is the sign of the zodiac in which the Moon resided at the time of your birth.

How were all the astrological forces or magnetic pulls of the planets aligned when you arrived here on Earth? I was born on April 4th, in spring, so am guided by the sign of Aries, the first zodiac sign. I was born at 5:50 a.m., when the Sun was rising. Because I was born at dawn in spring, my rising sign and sun sign are the same. Your rising sign is determined by the zodiac that was on the eastern horizon at the moment of your birth.

The Sun sign determines our ego and vitality and is considered the director of our astrological chart. A productive, happy life and positive identify are more easily realized when you are open to the influence of this overt planetary influence. It is who you are. Feel connected to

The Moon's influence on water movement and plants shifts subtly as it moves through the signs of the zodiac, but its beauty unfailingly calms our spirits. Photo by Diane Lasceski-Michaels

this significant guiding star (yes, the Sun is a star and not a planet) and trust its strength and steady course to guide you on our planet Earth. Since I am an Aries, my keynote is enthusiasm! I get really excited over starting projects and activities. Starting seeds is definitely my favorite gardening activity, along with making bouquets, the beginning of making a room more beautiful and energized.

The Moon sign is more inward and governs subconscious, emotional, or habitual responses. Throughout cultures and time, emotions are governed and symbolized by Water, and Water is governed by the Moon. According to Dr. William Davidson, a specialist on medical astrology, in his book *Davidson's Medical Lectures*, "The Sun is our natural voltage, and our Moon is our rate of flow." If you would like to learn your own Moon sign, you can find it out by having your birth chart generated online. You can find this information for free at many websites, such as www.astro.com.

If the Sun is a star, is the Moon a planet? Not really, according to the International Astronomical Union (IAU), although it acts like a planet, says lunar scientist Barbara Cohen. The current definition of a planet is a celestial body that orbits around the Sun, is nearly round in shape, and swoops up nearby debris into its orbit. Attracting cosmic debris demonstrates its gravitational pull.

The Moon's influence is subtler, and its reflective energy changes with each shift of the Moon from one sign to another as it moves through the zodiac. The signs of the zodiac each have a basic quality that relates to the four energetic elements of Fire, Earth, Air, and Water (more about the elements in chapter 3). Aries begins the cycle, in a hot Fire sign. Next comes Taurus, a cool but dry Earth sign; followed by Gemini, an Air sign; then comes the Water element in the sign of Cancer. This cycle continues—Fire, Earth, Air, Water—making a flowing cycle of dry and moist influences for various gardening and other activities throughout the months. This rhythm is made in heaven!

The continual shifts every two and a half to three days make for a wonderful system to complete all your gardening and life chores utilizing all-natural energies under the Sun: expanding, contracting, articulating, contemplating, sprouting, weeding, organizing, creating, and on and on it goes. Doors open and close, with various opportunities that are always shifting. Today plant, tomorrow weed and clean,

The Moon's Influence

I came across this beautiful quote from seventeenth-century astrologer William Lilly about what the moon governs in Lee Lehman's excellent reference guide, *The Book of Rulerships*:

> body, emotions, moods, changeability, memory, ethereal, habits, rhythms, down bearing, cold, moist and phlegmatic, organs with contained spaces, feelings, basic needs, your mother, mothering, yin, astrological sign of cancer, stomach, breasts, lungs, meninges of brain, all bodies of water, the stomach and the linings of internal organs, the moon rules round things, figures, like our bodies. Moon is related to Sulfur, Pluto, Monday is Moon Day, round vegetables, cabbages, pomegranate, coconuts, trailing plants such as melons, cucumbers, corn, salty things, milk and dairy products, sweets, pearls, emerald, moonstone, ducks, cranes, herons, silver metal and white color, Frogs, the Otter, Snails, Midwives, Nurses, Queens, Countesses, Ladies, all manner of Women; as also the common People, messengers, The Moon holds memories, even lifetimes ago, imprinting on mothers, the subconscious, our emotions, and psychology.

and then organize a couple days later. I have found success in all my chores by tuning in to this planetary rhythm.

My style of following the phases of the Moon and the influences of the elements is based on the traditional *Old Farmer's Almanac* style of lunar gardening. I have also begun weaving biodynamic methods into my practice, particularly the work of German biodynamic farmer and researcher Maria Thun. This methodology adds more dimensions to celestial gardening and provides another option when the timing may be off according to traditional method. This is OK. Play around with these methods. The point of this book is to get you to drop your ego and look for guidance from higher places. "I am going to do this today," becomes, "What energetic doors are open today and what is the best use of my power to create a better world?" I describe Maria Thun's method at the end of this chapter.

The most overt and visual sign of the Moon influencing life on Earth is the ocean tides. During the New and Full Moons, the tide is higher than the other two weeks of the month. Even though the Moon has no light of her own, holding the energy in, she governs the watery aspects of life on Earth. We are composed of around 60 percent water, so it stands to reason that as the Moon shifts the ocean tides, our bodies and emotions respond to her force. This reasoning would extend to plants as well, since most species are about 90 percent water.

Gazing at the Moon, night after night, we see her as a symbol of both changeability and rhythm. Like being rocked in a boat on gentle waves, the Moon offers her reassuring tempo, suggesting that just as things retreat and go away, new light is around the corner. The Moon holds the energy of yin, female energy described in Chinese medicine as the cool, dark side of the mountain. Yang is the sunny, dry, and hot side of the mountain, representing the outward male energy. Thinking in these terms helps you understand the energy of the Moon and what she governs.

The Phases of the Moon

Almanacs use two sets of descriptors to describe the Moon phases and they are both correct. One set of descriptors refers to the New Moon as the First Quarter, the waxing half Moon as the Second Quarter, the Full Moon as the Third Quarter, and the waning half Moon as the Fourth Quarter.

I use the other common set of descriptors for the Moon phases, the ones referred to by astrologer Steven Forrest in *The Book of the Moon*. The four phases are New Moon, First Quarter, Full Moon, and Last Quarter, as shown in the illustration of the moon's phases on page 30.

A clue to the Moon's phase or shape in the sky is the term *DOC*. The First Quarter Moon is shaped like the letter *D*—it is a semicircle with the curve on the right side. Then comes the Full Moon, a brilliantly lit O. In the Last Quarter, the Moon is shaped like a C, a semicircle with the curve on the left side. (You can also use the trick of raising your right hand and making a C shape. That shows you the First Quarter. Raise your left hand in a C and it shows the shape of the Last Quarter.) The waxing Moon is when the Moon appears to be growing larger, progressing from

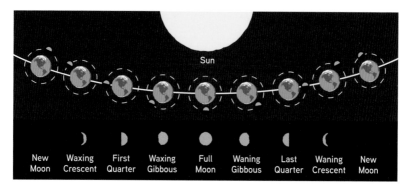

At the New Moon, when it is not in the night sky, the Moon is positioned between the Earth and the Sun. As it revolves around the Earth, it reaches Full Moon stage when the Earth is between the Sun and Moon and the Moon is in full light. Other Moon phases are the First Quarter (waxing from the half Moon), the Last Quarter (waning from the half Moon), and the crescent and gibbous phases. Illustration by Jerry Chapa

New Moon to Full Moon. The waning Moon appears to be shrinking, from Full Moon to New Moon. When the Moon is shaped like an egg, it is called a gibbous phase. The Balsamic Moon (or Waning Crescent) occurs right before the New Moon, when the Moon is a narrow crescent about to disappear, almost evaporating into thin air.

The most basic rule of thumb for gardening by the Moon is to plant aboveground crops as the Moon is waxing (increases from New until Full Moon) and plant below-ground crops as the Moon is waning (decreases from Full to New Moon).

There is more to consider, though:

* ★ Plants that produce seeds *outside* the fruit—such as lettuce, cabbage, and broccoli—are planted from the New Moon to the First Quarter.
* ★ Plants that produce their seeds *inside* the fruits—such as tomatoes and peppers—are planted from the First Quarter to the Full Moon.
* ★ Root crops are planted the week after the Full Moon.
* ★ The Last Quarter is for death, destruction, and wrapping things up, such as harvesting for storage, weeding, setting traps, and completing projects.

To fine-tune, we plant during moist influences: the Earth signs Taurus, Virgo (infertile, good for flowers), and Capricorn; and the Water signs Cancer, Scorpio, and Pisces. Harvesting and weeding are best during dryer phases: the Fire signs Aries, Leo, Sagittarius; and the Air signs Gemini, Libra, and Aquarius. Luckily, a watery sign switches to a dry sign every two and a half to three days, so you don't have to wait an entire week to switch to your next gardening chore.

Chapter 4 has details on the astrological signs and their influences.

When Does the New Moon Rise?

Almost no one knows when the New Moon rises. I have asked this question of hundreds of people when I give "Gardening by the Moon" presentations—audiences with many, many gardeners and Nature lovers. Only one person has ever known the answer, and he was an astrologer! A clue is, "When does the Full Moon rise?" Most of us have had the awe-inspiring experience of standing outside as the Sun sets in the west, watching a glorious Full Moon rise at the same time in the east. There's a sense of security in the alignment of the Sun, Earth, and

Moon Planning

New Moon (phase 1). Set intentions for this cycle and determine your plan.

Waxing Crescent (phase 2). Deepen your resolve.

First Quarter (phase 3). Take action, following the steps in your plan.

Waxing Gibbous (phase 4). Refine and improve your plan.

Full Moon (phase 5). Culminate and let realizations come to you.

Waning Gibbous (phase 6). Disseminate. Let go, and express new-found truths.

Last Quarter (phase 7). Seed your next cycle.

Balsamic Moon (phase 8). Dream into your intuition and instinct. Revere this time for renewal.

Moon—a feeling of "I am meant to be here and make my contribution or just feel the bliss of life!"

Yes, the Full Moon rises at sunset at six p.m. and sets at six a.m. And the new Moon rises at dawn and is up in the sky during the day. That is why we cannot see it!

The New Moon

The New Moon rises at six a.m. and sets at six p.m., at dawn and dusk, in the same arc as the Sun. At the New Moon, the Moon is between the Earth and the Sun. The Earth, Moon, and Sun form a nearly straight line. From Earth's perspective, the Sun and the Moon seem to be in the same place, or conjunct. The light of the Sun is hitting the "back" of the Moon, so to speak, and no visible reflected light from the Moon can be seen on Earth. This phase is depicted in almanacs as a black disk and is the point in each month when the Moon is nearest to the Sun.

The dark of the Moon is considered to be the first day of the Moon's cycle, and it is also called the Dead Moon. It symbolizes the point of endings and beginnings.

Each month the New Moon falls on the zodiac Sun sign for that month. For example, April's New Moon is always in the sign of Aries and August's New Moon is in Leo. Keep this in mind as you plan your month, knowing at each New Moon that the Moon's energy will be representing that month's zodiacal patterns.

You can also think ahead about the Moon's movement through the signs during that month, keeping in mind that the Moon moves into a new sign every two and a half to three days. From the time of the New Moon to the Full Moon, the Moon will move through six signs. For example, two weeks after the New Moon of Aries, the Moon will be in Libra, six signs away from Aries.

The New Moon is like the seed, resting and holding energy in. Something new, unique, dynamic, and deep is in the seed, and it wants to come out to beautify the world! Before watering and the influences of the elements move the seed to germinate, the best thing the seed can do is rest and hold energy in. This is the message of the New Moon phase. Think of it as the resting seed gathering energy to expand into the best version its genetics and surroundings offer. The day after the New Moon energy begins—think expansion!

As the Moon grows larger in appearance, gravitational pull is stronger. Elements that build up the body and strengthen it are favored in this quarter. It is a good time for speeding up the healing of wounds, too. Energy is increasing when the Water element is rising beneath the soil surface and moisture is high in the soil.

The water table is closest to the soil surface at the Full Moon, as the water rises. The next highest tide occurs at the New Moon. While this change is visible at the ocean's shores, this change is invisibly happening beneath the soil everywhere on Earth, too. Microbes, worms, and mycorrhiza are activated, and the soil awakes. The high water table benefits annuals planted directly in the soil.

The Waxing Crescent

The Waxing Crescent Moon appears approximately three and a half days after the New Moon, in the western sky after sunset. This minor phase is when the crescent grows toward a half Moon. A waxing moon reminds me of dipping candles, a primitive method of candle making, dipping a wick, again and again, into melted wax as it grows larger with each dip. The wick, the candle, a source of light, grows larger as you continue the process, just like a waxing moon.

The Crescent Moon appears approximately three and a half days after the New Moon and appears in the western sky after sunset. A crescent universally symbolizes and instills a feeling of newness and hope. Crescent comes from the Latin word *crescere*, meaning to increase or grow. This is a time to manifest your dreams. There will always be obstacles on your path, but the point of this time is to so strongly tap into your unique creativity and vision that you can let that dream crack through the barriers, like a seed breaking though the seed coat and sending out roots.

This is not easy for the seed, either! The seed has been dormant, with a tough seed coat to hold the life in. The seed must orient to the magnetic pull of the Earth, stabilizing itself first with the emerging root. Once the correct orientation is defined, the shoot emerges, heading toward the Sun. There may be days when a germinating seed is challenged by drought or stalled by flooding, but the determined root withstands obstacles and follows its destiny, solid and clear. Seeds do a great job of manifesting their destiny. Thankfully, they don't give up, wishing to be something else. They take their inner Sun and shine to the best of their ability, within the surrounding conditions. You can learn from seeds how to move through obstacles to manifest your inner calling to make your unique contribution to the world.

The First Quarter

The First Quarter begins when the Moon looks half full, with light on the right side (as in a *D*-shape), and lasts until the Full Moon. This phase rises at noon, sets at midnight, and lasts for about a week, getting bigger and bigger. It is day seven of the Moon's full cycle and is about a week after the New Moon. Through the coming week, it expands into the Full Moon.

The First Quarter is a time to manifest inspirations and take action to actualize your plan. It favors expansion and realizing goals. This is the best phase to sign big contracts, for growth. Signing contracts in the Waxing Crescent phase may be too expansive. The New Moon brings the energy of wonder, like a baby discovering everything for the first time. During the First Quarter, the energy gels and moves forward toward a constructive goal.

The Waxing Gibbous

This gibbous Moon is egg-shaped, growing from over a half moon into the full circle. The uneven egg shape brings unstable energy. Be aware: unexpected events may happen during this phase. Remember, it is not so much what happens but how you handle it. Be ready to adapt to change and find solutions that are good for all involved!

The Full Moon

At the time of the Full Moon, the Sun and Moon are on opposite sides of the Earth, with the Sun making the Moon glow its reflected brilliance. Why doesn't the Earth block the Sun's light from reaching the Moon during this phase? Because the Moon is five degrees off the ecliptic plane, peeking around the Earth and receiving the Sun's rays. (I explain this in more detail later in this chapter.)

What an amazing and compassionate creation to allow us to enjoy the light of Mother Moon through her path around the Earth. The Full Moon is the most obvious phase because it is out all night long.

Table 2.1 Names of the Full Moon

Month	Traditional Indigenous Name	Additional Names
January	The Wolf Moon	The Old Moon or Ice Moon
February	The Snow Moon	The Hunger Moon
March	The Worm Moon	The Crow Moon, Crust Moon, or Sap Moon
April	The Pink Moon	The Sprouting Grass Moon or Egg Moon
May	The Flower Moon	The Corn Planting Moon or Milk Moon
June	The Strawberry Moon	The Rose Moon or Hot Moon
July	The Buck Moon	The Thunder Moon or Hay Moon
August	The Sturgeon Moon	The Red Moon, Green Corn Moon, or Grain Moon
September	The Harvest Moon	The Full Corn Moon
October	The Hunter's Moon	The Travel Moon or Dying Grass Moon
November	The Beaver Moon	The Frosty Moon
December	The Cold Moon	The Long Night Moon or Oak Moon

Companion to the Sun, it is one of Earth's two bright lights, pulsing with life. The Full Moon rises at dusk and sets in the morning, beginning around day fourteen of the cycle. It lasts for about a week, until we see the Moon is half-lit and decreasing.

The mind is open and aware during the Full Moon. With heightened intuition, as I walk through my garden, certain plants will catch my attention over others. When they call to me like this, I pick these medicinal plants and bring them in to brew an infusion. Since I am familiar with these plants, I know how to use them and what benefits they offer. Read anything by Rosemary Gladstar for information on how to increase well-being with plants, both wild and cultivated.

The Waning Gibbous

The light has been shown to us all during the Full Moon. Now what are you going to do with that wisdom? Now the energy draws inward, and we can access archetypal knowledge and the perennial philosophy that encompasses all religions and spiritual traditions: focused on unity, compassion, love, and self-realization. Try to integrate the insights you received at the Full Moon into your life to bring in more depth and meaning to life for you and others.

Last Quarter

In this phase of completion, we see a half Moon, with light on the left side (as in the C-shape). The Last Quarter rises at midnight and sets at noon, beginning around day 21 of the cycle. The Moon wanes until it becomes the New Moon, seeming to disappear completely.

This is a time of rest, renewal, and death. All life energy is contained, therefore it is a good time for elective operations. From the New Moon to Full, this watery energy of the Moon supports outward action. The phase of the Last Quarter is a time to let go of what you created over the last two weeks. Observe, share it, and be happy you have contributed to a better world! In this phase, your new-found knowledge gets distilled and becomes richer. Take time to fine-tune your work and rejoice in your accomplishments and efforts. Use this quiet time of distillation to review what is accomplished and vision your next moves.

Balsamic Moon

This is when the Moon is a crescent, right before the New Moon. It is a time of stillness. The Moon's energy is decreased. It rises early in the morning, between four and six a.m.

The Balsamic Moon opens doors to visions and imagination. The spirit realm may become more real than this world. This is the time to access knowledge from your ancestors. Did any of them garden in the traditional way, according to planetary guidance? Perhaps they will offer you some wisdom during this time, when the veils are thin.

Traditionally made balsamic vinegar is stored in a cool, dark place for up to twelve years. Think about that dark time, aging and improving the quality of the vinegar. Hence we use the term *balsamic*.

❋   ❋   ❋

Every week offers beneficial influences for planting, harvesting, or weeding, but you may not get the exact alignment you are seeking every week. For example, Libra may not fall during the expanding Moon phases for flower planting; it may fall on a root or death week (after a Full Moon or Last Quarter). We just do what we can, observe the response to our actions, and experience joy, gaining knowledge in the meantime.

Gardeners know they are subject to Nature's laws. We plant after the frost-free date is passed, schedule planting around rain, harvest during expected drier times, and gather all the tender crops before the killing frost in fall. Why would a gardener question the larger influence of planetary influences beyond the Sun and Earth?

We are out of touch with our place on the planet as a culture, but the time is now to connect with that which sustains us. In gardening, you are joining forces with Nature. Nature follows cycles and rhythms. Roots grow downward, responding to the Earth gravity and rotation.

We see planetary influences in tides, which are higher during the Full Moon, and the Moon's influence is still listed in newspapers under "Best Fishing Days." This ancient practice of using the Moon's guidance for when to fish has very practical applications. My first observation with this practice set me into a rhythm of planting and weeding every week in spring, guiding me to not just fixate on my favorite thing in the world—planting every day.

The Ascending and Descending Moon

There is yet another nuance that could be integrated into your celestial gardening activities: the ascending and descending Moon phases. These terms refer to the arched pathway that the Moon travels around the Earth. As seen from Earth, the Moon travels on a plane that is 5.5 degrees offset from the ecliptic plane. This creates a gentle wave-like motion, from our perspective. Luna is said to be ascending as it moves north of the ecliptic and descending as it moves south of the ecliptic.

I have been planting according to the Moon's phases and astrological signs for over thirty years, but it is only recently that I learned about the implications of the ascending and descending Moon's influences for planetary planting. A self-proclaimed directional dyslexic, this concept was tricky for me to comprehend. The cyclic and shifting energy of the zodiac signs comes more naturally to my way of thinking, and of course, the Moon's phases are as obvious as turning on a light, if you live where the sky is noticeable.

> The earth breathes out in the morning and in again during the afternoon. During a wet weather period, evaporation of the moisture in the soil can be enhanced by hoeing in the morning of Flower days and Fruit days. During a dry period, the night moisture and dew formation can be increased by hoeing in the evening of Leaf and Root days.
>
> —**Maria Thun,** *Work on the Land and the Constellations*

Although I do not practice formal biodynamic farming, my path is linked with that of Austrian philosopher Rudolf Steiner (1861–1925) through the worldwide meditation group, TSG Foundation. This group studies world spiritual masters, including Alice Bailey (1880–1949). Steiner developed biodynamic agriculture in 1924. And both Bailey and Steiner brought the teachings of the Theosophical Society forward, although Steiner left that group and started the Anthroposophical Society in 1912. My goal aligns with Alice Bailey's group, the Lucis Trust. I seek to reconnect people to the rhythm of the universe to inspire them to return to Nature as a guide to restore order and consciousness to our dear planet. This study has helped me find answers that I had been looking for since I was a little Catholic girl who noticed that the teachings of that religion were very contradictory.

I do not know whether the concept of planting in sync with the ascending and descending Moon phases dates back before the time of Rudolf Steiner. Try it out when the traditional method does not suit your need for the day. (I simply *must* plant, harvest, fill in the blank . . . *today!*)

Maria Thun (1922–2012) was a biodynamic grower from Germany who devoted forty years to testing Steiner's biodynamic theory. She tested all the applications I mention in this book (Moon phases, astrological sign/sidereal cycle, and the ascending/descending Moon) and found the ascending and descending Moon was worth following. She also found that there is a daily ascending and descending rhythm. According to Thun:

> As regards the rhythm of the day, we also find an alternation of these two tendencies depending on the daily movement of the Earth. The ascending phase is from about 3 o'clock in the morning until about midday and the descending phase from 3 o'clock in the afternoon until well into the night.

As mentioned earlier, the Moon's 5.5-degree variance from the ecliptic plane around the Earth is the reason we can see the light of the Full Moon. If the Sun, Moon, and Earth were in perfect alignment in a single plane, we would not see any light reflected at the Full Moon. The Earth would block the Sun's light because the Earth is larger than the Moon. Knowledge of this cosmic plan makes me feel very loved and cared for, like being perfectly set in a big cosmic puzzle. What a lovely plan, to offer us these two lights, with this slightly off-center alignment allowing us to enjoy the show. I love what the Full Moon brings me:

Tropical vs. Sidereal Zodiac

This book and most Western astrologers use the tropical system of the zodiac, which is based on the Sun's apparent movement relative to the Earth. This is more accessible for the general gardener, in my opinion, because it starts with the vernal equinox, when the Sun crosses the celestial equator from south to north. It is based on the four seasons of the year. The twelve zodiac sections are divided into thirty degrees to fill the 360 degree circle.

The sidereal zodiac is based on the fixed stars. It begins with the fixed star Spica in the constellation of Virgo. Individual segments are not necessarily thirty degrees, because they correspond to the fixed stars' placement in the sky.

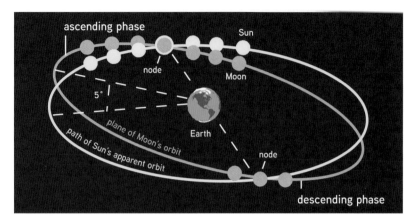

The plane of the Moon's orbit is about 5.5 degrees offset from the plane of the Earth's orbit. Thus, for two weeks each month, the Moon is ascending, and for the next two weeks, it is descending. When the Moon crosses the plane of the Earth's orbit (the nodes), an eclipse can take place. Illustration by Jerry Chapa

inspiration, excitement, and the ability to walk or ski at night or to get extra romantic. Thank goodness for this variation in the Moon's path!

A Note on the Nodes

Most of the time, the Moon is traveling above or below the ecliptic plane. This is why eclipses are so rare. Eclipses take place only when the Moon crosses the ecliptic plane and is exactly in alignment with the Sun and Earth. These occurrences are called the *lunar nodes*, and celestial energy is unsteady at these times. Therefore, it's best to avoid planting or taking any thoughtful action for results when the Moon is at a lunar node. Use the time for meditation, inspiration, journaling, and regeneration of your spirit instead.

For two weeks each month, the Moon's path climbs a little higher (ascends) above the horizon, and for the next two weeks, its path descends so that it appears closer to the horizon, just as the sun does in its yearly cycle. The Moon also has a yearly cycle with the ascending Moon running from winter to summer and the descending Moon traveling south of the ecliptic from summer to winter, as shown in the illustration of the orbit of the Moon on this page.

Let's follow the path of the Sun through the sky over a year from the Northern Hemisphere. Around Christmastime, the Sun is at its lowest point in its apparent motion around the Earth, the winter solstice, and it is in the sidereal zodiac sign of Sagittarius (or Tropical Capricorn) After the solstice, the Sun's path across the daytime sky gradually begins to ascend, giving us longer days. We see the point of sunrise moving from the southeast more toward the eastern sky a bit more every day. At the spring equinox, around March 21, the Sun is in the sign of Sidereal Pisces. It reaches the midpoint of its ascension, and the length of day and night are equal. The point of sunrise continues to move past due east toward northeast. At the summer solstice in mid-June, the Sun reaches its highest point and starts to descend. It continues to do so, shortening the days through the autumnal equinox of equal day and night, until winter solstice, and the cycle begins again.

Of course, it is not the Sun that is moving, but we perceive its path across the sky changing because of the Earth's tilt on its axis. For half the year, the northern Hemisphere is tilted toward the Sun, and for the other half of the year, the Southern Hemisphere is tilted toward the Sun, which is also why the seasons occur at opposite times of year in the two hemispheres.

As the Earth travels 360 degrees around the Sun, these ascending and descending influences last around five or six months, unlike the Moon's travel, which offers two weeks each month of ascending and descending influences. The exact time when the Moon crosses the ecliptic plane varies, so both Gemini (summer solstice in late May to late June) and Sagittarius (winter solstice in late November to late December) are times when the gardener will have to check to see where the Moon is, whether it is ascending or descending on its travel around the Earth.

Note: The following descriptions are for the Northern Hemisphere; they are opposite for the Southern Hemisphere.

Ascending Moon

Every month, the Moon passes in front of the constellations of Sagittarius, Capricorn, Aquarius, Pisces, Aries, Taurus, and sometimes Gemini, when in the ascending phase. An ascending Moon (ASC) path draws the sap of the plants upward, increasing vitality and enhancing the upper portions of a plant. This is a good time for grafting and for harvesting produce above ground. Cut flowers and fruits are said to last longer when harvested during this phase. The Moon reaches its

Table 2.2 Ascending and Descending Moon Activities

Ascending Moon	Descending Moon
the energy of winter and spring	the force of summer and autumn
harvest time	planting time: plant out seedlings
sap from soil moving upward	sap from soil moving downward
promotion of seed germination	good for transplanting, especially trees
harvest of above-ground plants and fruits; cutting flowers	harvest of medicinal flowers and root crops
grafting; cutting scion wood	pruning
higher vitality available for plants and gardeners	spreading compost, working soil
taking cuttings from trees or vines	getting rid of things, such as weed
picking fruit for storage	stimulation of roots with organic fertilizer or compost

highest point when in Gemini, at summer solstice, then it starts to descend. As it does so, the plants orientate themselves more toward their roots. If you are taking cuttings for grafting, it is good to do this at the ascending Moon so that the scions do not wilt so easily.

Descending Moon

A descending Moon (DSC) passes in front of the constellations of Gemini, Cancer, Leo, Virgo, Libra, and Scorpio, and sometimes Sagittarius. Sagittarius and Gemini can fall on either side of this phenomenon, so once again, check a celestial gardening calendar or almanac to determine when the Moon crosses the ecliptic, altering its force.

The descending Moon draws the sap down. Roots connect with the soil more easily because of this gentle tug, so it's a good time to plant or transplant seedlings. This is also a great time to apply organic fertilizer because the lunar pull helps escort it into the soil. Sap flow decreases at this time, so this is also a suitable period, if the season is right, for pruning trees and cutting hedges. Pruning topiaries, espaliers, fruit bushes, and fruit trees is particularly favored. To keep growth from sprouting back, fire signs should be chosen.

CHAPTER 3

The Four Elements

*God speaks through all things and all Nature is an open
book, if you but seek to read it.*

—Jalaluddin Rumi

The four elements of Fire, Earth, Air, and Water are the energetic building blocks for all life and matter. Understanding the elements helps us perceive how energy shifts through the days, months, and years. Picture warm spring winds (Air) melting away the snow (Water) to allow Sun (Fire) to dry the ground (Earth) as the winter shifts into spring. The word *element* has multiple meanings, but I am not using it in the sense of chemical elements (as in the periodic table of the elements).

In terms of modern physics, fire is plasma, earth (as in soil) is solid, air is gas, and water is liquid. But in the framework of celestial gardening, we work with what are known as the *classical elements* or *archetypal elements*, or even as *temperaments*. This has to do with understanding physical matter in terms of the qualities of hot, dry, moist, and cool. These energies can be perceived on physical, emotional, and spiritual levels. These patterns are repeated in many familiar modalities, from various cultures throughout time, including the Native American Four Directions, Jungian psychology, and eclectic herbalism.

Fire, Earth, Air, and Water dance together to form life both subtle and overt. What would Fire burn without the Earth and Air? What would hold Water without the Earth and evaporation of the Sun and wind moving clouds? How could Earth survive without Fire changing the chemistry of atoms, water making plants grow, and all of life supported by the Air?

This was in my mind when I decided to rename my company Four Elements Organic Herbals after fifteen years of calling it Nature's Acres. The change came about when I moved back to Wisconsin after living for six years in Texas. I attempted to incorporate under the name Nature's Acres, but there was another Nature's Acres already registered in Wisconsin. About that same time, I was learning about the four fundamental elements in my meditation class, and I realized Four Elements would be a good name for my company. It sounded more contemporary, not so 1980s. And I have such a strong affinity for fours, being born on the fourth day of the fourth month and on the forty-fourth parallel. There are many squares in my astrological chart, too, so the name would represent who I am and what I do very well. Hot (Fire, or Sun) and cold (Earth), moist (Water) and dry (Air) are the influences that cocreate my herb plants and products and that govern my activities in the greenhouse and fields, as well as in conversations and many other areas of my life. Note: In some classifications Earth is dry and Air is moist. Not so with the elements assigned to gardening.

Understanding the elements and their influences is essential because these are key components for celestial gardening practices. Who doesn't want better outcomes from their energy outputs? Therefore, we consider which element is having a strong influence on a particular day, and we allow that element to nudge our choice of activities in the

Table 3.1 The Four Elements: Qualities and Influences

Element	Zodiac Signs	Plant Correspondence
Fire	Aries, Leo, Sagittarius	fruit or seed
Earth	Taurus, Virgo, Capricorn	root
Air	Gemini, Libra, Aquarius	flower
Water	Cancer, Scorpio, Pisces	leaves

right direction. Remember, the basic approach of celestial gardening is to plant, transplant, and propagate under moist influences (Water and Earth signs) and to cultivate, harvest, and dehydrate for storage under dry influences (Air and Fire signs).

Fire

The Sun (Fire) brings life to all. Nothing would be here without the Sun, the magnificent beauty that makes people smile when it pops out from behind the clouds. Sun, shining on the green leaves of plants, powers photosynthesis and the cascade of sugars that plants produce as food. Plus, photosynthesis then provides the oxygen (Air) for other life forms to inhale. Like the Sun, Fire brings optimism, activities, and new beginnings. It is not the Sun/Fire's vision to plan the details of the job but to get things started. Fire is active and moves quickly.

Fire has great strength. It gets to the core of things and can transform matter. Defying gravity, Fire initiates and is innovative, creative, and enthusiastic.

Fire works well with Air, and my Fire is fueled by the Airy spirit of my Gemini husband, David. When we first started farming in the Baraboo Bluffs, the only plants on the land other than grass were a few green ash trees. Over time, our farm has become a botanical sanctuary for so many people, plants, animals, and birds. We have created an amazing organic farm from an open palette.

Physical States of Matter	Garden Activities	Temperaments	Season
plasma or combustion	cultivation and harvest	choleric	summer
solid	planting days and root days	melancholic	autumn
gases	cultivation, harvest, and flower days	sanguine	spring
liquid	planting days for most leafy plants and herbs	phlegmatic	winter

My Fiery Aries Spirit

I would not have begun or continued my business without my fiery, impulsive double Aries spirit. When an idea occurred to me, I just did it. (Impulsive Fire.) No business plan, and no far-reaching goal. I simply wanted to be at home with my young children and have a farm-based business. I started growing potted herbs for transplants because that is what I loved. I did not think (Air) how impractical that was (Earth). From there, I found that making wellness products based on the herbs was a better way to earn a living (go with the flow, Water). I have seen my fiery spirit jump into all kinds of projects, with the help of my Earth sign (my Moon is in Capricorn). I have been led to secure goals, not clearly set at the beginning. Still, I cannot think of anyone else who would stick with a business like Four Elements Organic Herbals for forty years, except for herbalist Deb Soule, the founder of Avena Botanicals in Maine. Inspired by the beauty of the plants, we keep our businesses going despite the intense pressure of FDA audits.

It is easy to conclude that the FDA favors the pharmaceutical corporations, which aim to intimidate herbal product companies, as if we could cut into their profits. Once while I was in the midst of a three-day inspection by two FDA agents, I saw on the news that there was a chemical spill upriver from the capital of West Virginia, with chemical contamination that ruined the water quality for many municipalities. Curious, I investigated what regulations were violated and what the repercussions would be for the polluting company. What I found was there were almost no regulations for these chemical companies and rarely significant fines! As an herb grower, I must undergo more scrutiny than companies that operate trains hauling loads of toxic chemicals through neighborhoods and near waterways.

Nonetheless, Deb and I and goal-oriented herbalists like us move forward with a common vision of serving humanity by providing pure herbal wellness, straight from the garden. (Deb also practices gardening by the Moon as part of her own bio-dynamic practice). Perhaps following astral guides has helped us maintain our businesses for so many years, assisted by the energy of the elements, too.

Fire in the body rules all things hot, like the acids of digestion. Fire also rules the sight and the eyes, associated with its light-giving energy. When toxic, Fire is impatient and angry. Fire is hot, dry, and light, and reduces the coldness of the other elements.

In Fire, we can find the Violet Flame Invocation using this color of transmutation. This esoteric meditation uses the color violet that occurs in fire flames and focuses on transmuting negative energy into positive outcomes for everyone involved. Fire is very transformative.

Violet Flame Meditation

Find a quiet spot where you can collect your physical, emotional, and mental bodies. Visualize a violet flame surrounding you, starting at your feet, circling your body up to your head. Imagine the flame burning away any negative energy or emotions you are holding on to, like fear, anger, or sadness. You can hold onto and empower your meditation by repeating a mantra during this process, like " Purify me, violet flame; I release negativity into the violet flame" or "I am purified by the violet flame." Feel the shift! An important aspect of this is that the energy does not just go away, it is transmuted into something else, so it cannot come back and haunt you again, just like flames burn things into a totally different form.

Fire-inspired daily mantra: "Using the light permeating my whole nature, I take any difficult situation and see the best possible outcomes for all involved."

Earth

Earth, via the soil, springs forth life, with the help of the Sun (Fire) and Air. Our farm has received so much organic matter, labor, and love, and returns to us so much abundance. Most of our food, medicine, and my livelihood are sourced from our spot here on Earth. Beauty surrounds us with both native and horticulturally selected gardens. (Soil is what we grow plants in: dirt is what is in your vacuum cleaner.)

Partnering with Earth has been a most revealing career. In fact, the more I study plants and agriculture, the more I realize how much I do not know. Plants keep you humble. From the vantage point of an herbalist, plants are being studied more and more. It is fascinating to be able to reach back in time and read about traditional uses of plants, and then to fast-forward to modern biochemical research that describes the metabolic pathways through which healing compounds from plants can assist living organisms. I understand more deeply the interconnections as I see how the subtle energies of the planets affect the plants I grow, which in turn affect the health of living things. It makes so much sense to me that medicine grows abundantly from the Earth, just like food and building materials—all the essentials.

I have always been happy to get up in the morning and begin my day of working with plants. I prefer their mostly quiet nature to the unsettled spirits that I would encounter working with human patients or clients. I find so much comfort in Nature's embrace and enjoy a career where I work outside cultivating plants through the seasons. Don't misunderstand, plants can be just as demanding as any upset person. I often feel like they are the bosses and I must obey! "Plant me now, my root ball is choking me, water me or else I am dead, harvest today or lose it!" I hear their ultimatums very clearly.

Earth is resourceful. Nature hates a void and will fill any empty spaces with plants that will loosen and energize the soil. If you have an empty spot in your yard, you better plant something you want there, or Nature will choose for you! You may have an interesting surprise, but most likely the plant sprouting is something you are battling with elsewhere.

Earth represents the energy of all material matter. My vantage point of Earth is that she is Goddess-like and abundant. It is June as I write this, and I can step outside and collect food—lettuce, parsley, spinach, and nasturtium blossoms. Plus, we still have stored onions, potatoes, carrots, beets, and garlic from last year's harvest. Most days I harvest tea herbs. Today's blend is tulsi (*Ocimum sanctum*) and sage (*Salvia officinalis*). I pick bouquets to inspire and uplift my soul. Sensational iris is blooming today—I call them the orchids of the North. I collect medicine for use all year, not just for myself and family but for all my customers. Hawthorn (*Crataegus oxyacantha*) is blooming today, and I will collect the flowers, which are higher in flavonoids than the fruits. We are also

Beauty is the most powerful force in the universe.

processing lovage (*Levisticum officinale*) and garden angelica (*Angelica archangelica*). The Moon is in Aries in the Last Quarter (a good time to harvest for storage, as I explain later in this chapter). It may sound idyllic, and it is, because I love plants so much, but they are my bosses!

Earth is reliable, somewhat less so with climate change, but I believe she is predictably going outside common boundaries as we push her to extremes. We can count on the four seasons to come and go as the Earth orbits around the Sun, and on sunrise and sunset every day as the Earth rotates on its axis. She provides the palette for all plants to grow and photosynthesize, partnering with the Sun (Fire), Air, and Water.

In this love affair with Earth, my concern grows for the condition of our resources as I see our government offer less and less protection for them. Our culture is so removed from honoring the Earth, there is no second thought of dumping poison on that which sustains us. Nature's Bill of Rights gives me hope. "Rather than treating nature as property under the law, rights of nature acknowledges that nature in all its life forms has the right to exist, persist, maintain and regenerate its vital cycles," states the Global Alliance for the Rights of Nature.* There is a slow but steady movement asserting that because the Earth is alive, she deserves rights just as all living things. Think: birds, fish, and butterflies all have the same rights as people to pursue life, liberty, and happiness. Women and people of color used to be considered property by law, and these concepts are atrocious to consider now. Perhaps in my lifetime, we can treat other forms of life as equal and honor other forms of beauty and life that share this Earth, honoring the wisdom long held by Indigenous peoples of the Earth.

Earth is practical. She supplies habitat, food, water, and medicines for all beings, providing humans do not take more than their share. The World Wildlife Fund estimates we are losing between 20 and 200 species of plants and animals every day. Habitat loss to make way for greed creates imbalances and yields disease and mental anguish in our society. There is no "away" where we can dump chemicals and garbage, nor resources other than those provided on Earth (that were meant to sustain us all). We are in a closed system.

---

* "What Are the Rights of Nature?," Global Alliance for the Rights of Nature, https://www.garn.org/rights-of-nature.

Earth is sensual. She is cool, dark, and yin, which holds the mystery of life. We are all seduced by Nature's beauty.

Those governed by or tapping into the astrological influences of Earth can be conscious of suppling their Earthly needs. They will find security collecting things that offer comfort. So, under an Earth influence, it is a good time to use your resources wisely and collect things that make your life more comfortable, secure, and happy.

Earth-inspired daily mantra: "I see what is before me and with it, I create beauty and goodness for all."

Air

The Air element arrives as warm spring breezes that thaw the soil and dry it to a friable state. Soil is *friable* when a handful of it forms a ball when gently squeezed but crumbles easily if more pressure is applied. This is the perfect time for preparing the soil for planting. The Air brings freshness and newness and connects us all.

The element of Air has no structure or form but holds and supports communication and ideas and much more. It is through this ether that our intuition flows. Before anything becomes material, it must begin as an ephemeral idea or inspiration.

We can conjure up our dreams by releasing them into the air. An ancient quote from the Old Testament, Hebrews 11:1, states, "Faith is the substance of things hoped for and the evidence of things not seen." I love the mystery that Air holds and hope to catch my messages from afar through this supernatural source.

I have heard many stories of loved ones passing but the spirit returning in the lightness of a bird from above. The energy of that person is held in that bird, offering companionship, for days, weeks, and years afterward. Birds hold the element of Air, and the auspicious energy of the otherworld, with their songs and lightness.

At our farm, we honor the element Air and the birds by maintaining a habitat for the rare bobolink. The beautiful bobolink, with their

We feel the influence of the element of Air very strongly on summer evenings at our farm, especially with David's added Air/Gemini influence of continually beautifying and grooming our land.

"inverted tuxedo" arrangement of feathers, needs large open grasslands in which to nest. This habitat has been greatly reduced due to the common practice of cutting hay fields three times per year. Traditionally, hay was cut later in the season, after bobolinks had nested. So, we wait till after the fourth of July to cut our hay, providing the bobolinks time to raise their young until they are fledglings and leave the nest, before the whirling blades of farm machinery invade the fields.

Air carries qualities but has no substance of its own. It is the carrier for the electricity that moves the other energies. Air rules communication. In fact, think of recently outdated telephone wires that are replaced by wavelengths. This electromagnetic spectrum holds all Wi-Fi and cellphone use. Although all of this travels through the air, there is much discussion about this interfering with our ability to receive our intuitive guidance. Its movement is upward and circulating. It is light and dry. That is certainly the case in America's heartland, where we have temperature extremes ranging from 105 to –40°F (41 to –40°C)with winds shifting over the days and seasons. In the spring, we welcome these winds that dry the soil so we can get out and prepare the soil for planting.

In the body, Air governs hollow tubes or spaces, including blood movement in the veins.

Air-inspired daily mantra: "I receive all my guidance clear as a blue sky to express goodness in all contacts and move confidently forward. Directed with my heart, all my communications reach the best possible outcome."

Water

Water is a key element in gardening. Water partners with Earth and Fire to provide food, medicine, and supplies for shelter by powering the process of photosynthesis in plants. I write these words in early June, after all our transplants have recently been set in the field, not yet rooted in the surrounding soil, and temperatures are rising to the upper 80s with gusty winds. This is a challenge for the leaves of my lemon verbena, lemongrass, holy basils, and other tender transplants. Today we are in the Last Quarter, a time to review and finish up projects, and the Moon is in the sign of Taurus, so mulching is the perfect gardening activity. We will be preserving the moisture in the soil, keeping the competition from weeds down (which also helps preserve the Water element), and finishing up the planting process.

Water is the opposite of Fire, with its cold, wet, and heavy nature. In the body, water softens and moisturizes that which is too dry: joints, skin, and inflexible areas of the temperament. Water has excellent memory, and holds what is added to it, as can be seen in our polluted waterways. Just as Fire looks ahead, Water looks back.

Water provides much comfort. The sound of running water soothes, and a bath or shower is one of the simplest pleasures. A large glass of pure water can relieve anxiety (try this the next time you are feeling unsettled or upset; the effect is remarkable) and is basic to our survival.

Reassuring water can flow around obstacles, can shift matter to release blockages. This can happen on the physical level but also the emotional level.

Water rules emotions. No wonder controlling emotions is a super-power and is considered the second level of human evolution. Think of flooded dams: uncontrolled bursts of emotions have caused many lost friendships. Controlled emotions can heal. What is your choice? The trick is to control your emotions without inhibiting them. I find when involved in a difficult situation, if I reorient my heart in love, it is much easier to come to an understanding. If you aim to ready yourself to life's surprises, it may be easier to not become too excited, overwhelmed, or depressed when the unexpected occurs. Obstacles are an integral part of life. To inspire you even more than learning that simple water is there for calming our emotions, being solemn is a great magnet for divine energy. Try it when you need to attract positive influences in your life.

Like air, water moves and connects us all. While the oceans, lakes, and rivers hold the water, eventually it evaporates, creating clouds that rain the recycled water back to Earth. When you add organic matter to the soil, it absorbs water and holds it in place, preserving moisture for the plants' roots to tap into over time. This goes along with the theory that water has a memory; it holds on. Moist and dry relate to movement by contracting and expanding as they shift along this continuum.

According to Maria Thun's work, plants of which we eat the leaves should be sowed, hoed, and cultivated on leaf days, that is, on a Water sign (Cancer, Scorpio, Pisces). She also found that onions could be sown on leaf days if they were to be eaten fresh in the summer and not stored. Her research also showed that leaf development was stronger with plants sown when the Sun is in Pisces, that is February 19 to March 20.

But for later crops of greens, she recommends planting when the Sun is in Cancer, June 21 to July 22, when the Moon is also in a Water sign.

> **Water-inspired daily mantra:** "I am open to all surprises and can recognize and be guided, but not governed, through my emotions with joy and ease by reorienting my heart to love."

Celestial Cycles: The Elements, or the Triplicities

Now that you have a basic understanding of the four elements, let's study how they relate to the practice of gardening by the Moon. Each of the twelve zodiac signs relates to one of the four elements, and these groups of signs are called *triplicities*, having three signs apiece. The Fire signs are Aries, Leo, and Sagittarius; Earth signs are Taurus, Virgo, and

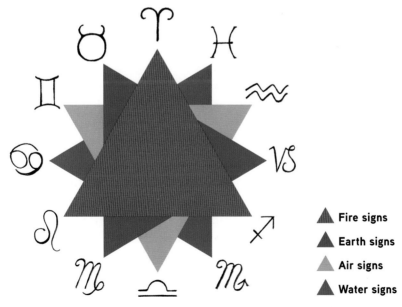

Here, the astrological signs are grouped as the triplicities, according to their connection to the elements of Fire, Earth, Air, and Water.

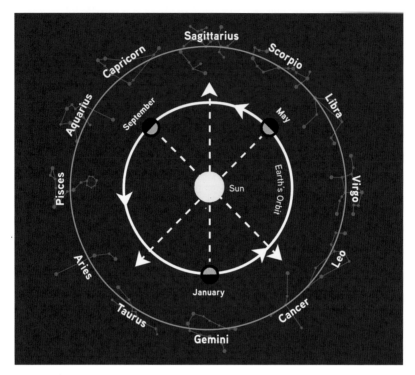

As the Earth revolves around the Sun, the Sun appears to move from one constellation to the next, from month to month. Illustration by Jerry Chapa

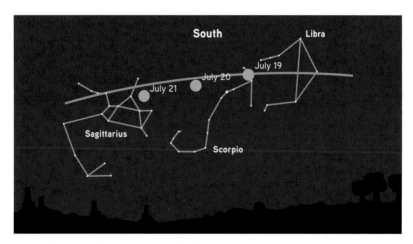

As the Moon revolves around the Earth, it appears to progress through the twelve constellations in one month's time. Here, we see the progress of the Moon from Libra through Scorpio and into Sagittarius. Illustration by Jerry Chapa

Capricorn; Water signs are Cancer, Scorpio, and Pisces; and Air signs are Gemini, Libra, and Aquarius.

Thinking in terms of these categories, the elements, or triplicities, can help you group the signs into their elemental forces. For example, Fire signs are all hot and drying. The Water signs are all moist and cooling. These principles hold true for people, plants, and the energy of a day.

You can see this in the illustration of the triplicities on page 55. The energy of a grouping of four—like the four elements—is tense and unstable, not as steady as the energy of threes. (Think of how common triangles are in the designs of load-bearing parts for buildings, such as roof trusses). Squares in an astrological chart are said to be an indication of a more challenging life, but squares also cause action because the number four holds the energy of creating life. People with squares in their charts are creative change-makers. They understand the saying, "The only thing constant in life is change." People with calm and peaceful triangles are more at ease, but with ease, why change things?

The series of triplicities repeats three times each year for the Sun and three times every month for the Moon. This is the aspect of astrology that answers the common question, "What sign are you?" From our perspective on Earth, the Sun appears to move in front of each zodiac sign once a year, remaining in front of that constellation for about one month. We also see the Moon and all the planets in our solar system pass in front of these constellations over varying spans of time.

Although each Sun sign dominates a span of about 30 days, that time span does not run from the first to the thirtieth of a standard calendar month. The range shifts through the months and years because, as explained in chapter 2, it takes less than the number of a days in a calendar month for the Moon to complete a full cycle through the zodiac. The sequence, as ever, is Fire, Earth, Air, Water, beginning with the Fire sign of Aries in the spring (March 21).

The Three Modes, or Quadruplicities

Another way to divide astrological signs is by their modality (or mode), or how they express their energy (details below). The three modalities are cardinal, fixed, and mutable. A group of four signs that have the same modality is called a *quadruplicity*. Knowing the manner of energy and creativity associated with each mode can help you decide the best activity for each day, whether you plan to spend the day in the garden or around your house or pursuing your career. If you need extra energy to get a project started, you'll want to choose a date when a cardinal sign is in force. If an activity needs sustaining motivation, a fixed sign is favorable. When the flexibility to move between energy that is fixed or initiating would be helpful, a mutable sign is the best match.

Cardinal Signs

The cardinal signs are considered initiators of new creations and beginnings—they bring in the new seasons. Aries brings in spring, Cancer begins summer, Libra opens autumn, and Capricorn starts winter. Cardinal signs possess the vital force that holds the first spark of a plan. These bring shifts of energy and momentum forward with lots of enthusiasm.

Aries brings leadership and control; Cancer favors home, emotions, and family; Libra brightens social relationships and partnerships; and Capricorn relates to a steady push toward material stability. How could a gardener use cardinal signs for auspicious starts?

Aries is the ultimate initiator, bringing in spring with the energy of Fire, as in the extended day lengths of spring. Do you feel your fingers reaching spontaneously for seeds in the spring, almost vibrating with excitement? I do. This energy cannot be contained, it must be released to begin projects. Who doesn't get inspired by spring? It brings such joy here in the dark and cloud-filled Great Lakes states. Daffodils and tulips emerge, their glorious brightness triumphing over mud season. The way I feel when I can finally spend time outdoors after a winter indoors makes me understand the energy of a headstrong, mountain-climbing ram or ewe charging to the top with no barriers observed. Begin projects and jump into action during an Aries Moon— the details can come later. When in charge, I would plan meetings on an Aries Moon. Business deals could be favored in instances where the other party needs to see you as a leader and in control.

Cancer, as a cardinal Water sign, is the number-one choice for starting seeds. What is more initiating than a seed? Cancer holds the momentum to create and nourish life. Planting your landscape with flowers and perennials to beautify your home would flow smoothly under this Cancer Moon. Cancer Moon people love their cozy homes. Planting vegetables would be fitting under a Cancer Moon with the intention of fostering health derived from homegrown produce.

A **Libra** Moon is a great time for throwing parties or planning a gathering in your garden to foster community and partnerships. Harvest your crops, prepare them into delicious and beautifully displayed dishes to share. The cardinal air sign, Libra desires balanced communication and initiates the Air qualities of observation and abstract contemplation, all beneficial factors for making connections. Plus the lighthearted quality pulls joy out of thin air.

Capricorn is the cardinal Earth sign and is a favorable sign for starting seeds, planting root crops (especially during the Last Quarter), and initiating garden and farm activities or other activities that build and control the material environment. Capricorn rules farms, along with Taurus. This is the best sign during which to put in fence posts, drawing energy to the Earth. Capricorn is the steadiest of the impulsive cardinal signs. Picture the goat: step by step, they make it to the top of the mountain, with their hooves firmly secured on Earth.

Fixed Signs

The fixed signs follow the cardinal signs in each quadruplicity. They represent the season's keynote: they sustain what is already created and do not bring in new energy. They land in the middle of each season. They are fixed in their representation of themselves, with stability and deep-rooted firmness. The fixed signs are Taurus (spring), Leo (summer), Scorpio (autumn), and Aquarius (winter). These signs hold together the energy of ideas and plans for fruition. People born under these fixed signs can hear of a plan and bring the project from start to finish.

As gardeners, how can we best use these energies for increased productivity? Taurus is tenacious and rules collection of things. Leo brings the fixed sun energy. Use this when you or your project needs to shine. Use Scorpio to gather the details of a project or you need intensity to bring a project to fruition. (Maybe plant peppers under a Scorpio Moon for extra heat!) Airy Aquarius is about gathering people to foster ideas and idealism.

Taurus, the bull or cow, represents the middle of spring, with seeds established and getting on their way (depending on your zone). A

Taurus Moon fosters material comfort and stability. Projects that deserve single-minded attention, especially to reach a material goal, are favored here. This fixed Earth sign is about making a lovely garden and enjoying it. Taurus energy does not like to go far and basks in the beauty and bounty of Earthly delights. Invite friends over for a garden tea party or plan a sensual moment with your love in the garden. Write your blog, newsletter, or promotional material for your farm under a Taurus Moon.

A **Leo** Moon brings the enthusiasm of Fire but with the sustained energy of a fixed sign. Leos integrated Fire into itself and can use its sunny personality to move a project forward. Use the Leo Moon to move *you* toward your goals. Visualization can be an important first step to reaching your goals, so picture the lion holding fast to its territory, resourceful and smart, and protecting its pride. The momentum is here!

Scorpio holds deep emotions and is meticulous with details. Scorpio, as a Water sign, is a good time for planting seeds. If you are an organic grower, use this idealistic passion to complete your paperwork to renew your certification, or other projects that require a strong desire for the end goal to sustain the effort of plowing through annoying and time-consuming red tape. (Although a Scorpio may enjoy this.)

Aquarius, governed by Air, is intellectual but fixed in opinion. This Moon would be a good time to hoe your garden while expanding your thoughts to craft your position on a subject you need to defend. This is when I would write a letter to the editor of my local newspaper stating why we should learn alternative methods of farming and gardening and eliminate the use of glyphosate and other cancer-causing chemicals allowed in our food systems.

Mutable Signs

The mutable signs come last in the series. They occur when one season morphs into the next and so are more changeable. Mutable signs are not single-minded. Their strength is that they can shift easily and are flexible and resilient. The mutable signs are Gemini (wraps up spring), Virgo (completes summer), Sagittarius (ends autumn), and Pisces (concludes winter).

How could a gardener utilize the flexibility of a mutable sign for betterment?

Gemini, an Air sign, is all about communication and gathering information. If you need curiosity or a nudge to open your mind to new possibilities, this is a good sign to work with. For example, it might

Moon in Virgo is a favorable sign for working on garden design and other projects that focus on beauty and flowers. Photo by Diane Lasceski-Michaels

be the best time for me to ponder the increasingly demanding details of running a certified-organic farming business. My dedication to organic farming is religious, but getting called out by certifiers because David and I collected bat guano from an attic and used it on our plants (that's not allowed because we couldn't produce a product label for the guano to insert in my recordkeeping file) is annoying at the least. The Gemini Moon will help me expand my views and open my mind to include these escalating requirements so I can maintain a happy partnership with my organic certifier.

Virgo brings in beauty and love, in its changeable forms. Use this power to change your surroundings or partnerships to enhance beauty. Remember, Virgo is an Earth sign, so a Virgo Moon is a good time for planting, but not for crops that you want to be fruitful. Why no fruit? Because Virgo represents the virgin. Her beauty and grace will enhance flower and vine growth. This Moon would assist in working on garden design, especially in a waxing Moon, and on working in the garden to enhance the beauty at a waning Moon.

Sagittarius is a Fire sign and opens you to a continually adaptive view of things. This mutable sign's keynote is observation. Sagittarius unifies the initiation of Aries, takes the internalization of Fire in Leo and brings the integrated ideas forth to better an idea. This may be a good sign (along with Gemini) to investigate enhancing your growing techniques with new techniques such as companion planting, and alternative pest and weed control measures. A Sagittarius Moon is recommended for camping or going outdoors to observe and expand your mind into the great horizonless horizon.

Pisces is a mutable Water sign and governs emotions. Pisces is also a good planting sign, favoring leafy growth. It is deep and thoughtful, like the fish in the ocean. This may be a good sign to explore any issues with working partners to gain a deeper understanding, to be sensitive to them and how the conversation is going.

It is fascinating to reflect on how the zodiac signs fit together with the elements as triplicities and quadruplicities, revealing the complexity of this framework. In the next chapter, I delve into each of the twelve zodiac signs to describe how their nuances can potentize our gardening efforts.

CHAPTER 4

The Astrological Signs and Their Influences

An image of the Zodiac is imprinted upon the Earth.

—JOHANNES KEPLER

I f the Moon phases are like the slow-moving hour hand of a clock, the astrological signs are like the faster-sweeping minute hand. As described in chapter 2, each Moon phase lasts about a week, but the influence of each astrological sign lasts only two and a half to three days. This nuance holds the personality of the day, so to speak, and can guide us on how to approach our day; is it an outward day, an inward day, an organizational day, a playful day? Knowing this will help you understand why some activities can be so difficult on certain days but proceed smoothly on others.

Learning about how each astrological sign holds power or personality helps in understanding how that sign can influence life. After all, the inherent energy existed before early astrologers designated symbols to each energy shift, so it makes sense that they assigned a symbol that matched the type of energy perceived. Reflecting on the quality of a symbol's energy can clarify why particular garden activities are assigned to that sign.

I ascribe to the motto Symbolism Is Real when studying astrological signs. I hope you will try it, too. If you are lucky, this attitude will grow into a practice you can play with whenever you are outdoors in Nature. "Is that bird telling me to be more playful? Did that squirrel just remind me it's time to do some harvesting?"

This schematic groups the signs according to the four elements and also to the four categories of garden plants: root, fruit, leaf, and bloom. Illustration by Jerry Chapa

As discussed in chapter 2, because the Moon orbits around the Earth once a month, it passes in front of all twelve astrological signs during that time, changing its zodiac sign every two and a half to three days. Another basis of celestial gardening is that the influences of the constellations mediate impulses on the Earth. From this understanding, I lead you in this chapter on a journey through each astrological sign to better understand their influences.

Note: The descriptions I use here for the signs focus on their influences for gardening activities. You'll also find descriptions of the signs in chapter 10, but there I focus on how the influence of a gardener's Sun sign affects their lives.

For each sign, I offer a few keywords to provide insight. When it comes to the Sun sign, the "quality" describes whether it begins a season, is in the middle of the season, or is moving toward the next season. This reflects the energy of cardinal carrying initiative, fixed being steadfast, and mutable holding more flexibility. Understanding these nuances opens more insights into how these signs open and close various forms of energy. Next, I mention the ruling element, followed by the ruling planet with a descriptive word or phrase to help you understand the designated planet. Throughout time astrologers have associated plants and herbs with the various signs, and I mention a few of those for each, too. The color of a sign is an indicator of how the sign expresses itself. Think in terms of the classic qualities of colors: red is fiery, blue is cooling, and so on.

Aries ♈ *The Ram*

Keywords: courageous, enthusiastic, initiating
Quality: cardinal
Element: Fire
Planet: Mars—energetic, impulsive, willing to fight for a cause
Plants: cabbages, peppers
Herbs: ginger (*Zingiber officinale*), nettles (*Urtica* spp.), red clover
(*Trifolium pratense*), St. John's wort (*Hypericum perforatum*),
wild geranium (*Geranium maculatum, G. robertianum*)
Color: red

The fiery sign of Aries is dry and barren. Aries, like other Fire signs, rules seeds and fruits. Because of Aries's hot and dry nature, it is one of the best signs for cultivating, eliminating pests, hoeing, and weeding. Prune fruit trees and shrubs under this dry phase to prevent regrowth. This sign also favors harvesting of fruit and root crops, and harvesting crops you plan to dry.

The exuberant push of Aries can also be useful when you want to encourage a crop to reach its mature stage faster than usual. Market gardeners can use this as a secret tool in timing the sowing of seeds. Lettuce can bolt quickly under an Aries Moon, but this could be used to your advantage in the case of sowing early lettuce for a quick harvest.

From autumn to early spring, the Moon is in Aries only during the waxing phase. Aries occurs in a waning phase during the typical grow-ing season in the Northern Hemisphere. The waning moon also favors weeding and cultivation, so the Moon in Aries is a strong influence for the gardener to follow.

Taurus ♉ *The Bull or Cow*

Keywords: determined, earthy, home-loving
Quality: fixed
Element: Earth
Planet: Venus—joy-seeking, sensual
Plants: apples, grapes, peas, potatoes, spinach
Herbs: coltsfoot (*Tussilago farfara*), feverfew (*Tanacetum parthenium*),
    mallows (Malvaceae family), all roots
Color: green

As a fixed Earth sign, Taurus is a joy for gardeners. With its earthy, feminine nature, the Moon in Taurus is productive and moist, and favors leafy or root crops and hardiness. The Venus rulership would benefit leafy things, making them more beautiful, while the Earth influence would favor root crops. The body part associated with Taurus is the neck, and short, sturdy growth under its influence displays the nature of the bull symbol. This

These young baikal skullcaps (*Scutellaria baicalensis*) were sown during Taurus, the fixed Earth sign, in the Last Quarter—the perfect time for sowing crops grown for their roots. Notice the labels that specify date (4/24) and the icons for the Moon sign and phase.

could be the ideal time for planting cut flowers, lettuce, and other leafy vegetables. In fact, all bulbous plants can do well sown with a Taurus influence. Taurus is one of the best signs for planting in general, so see if you can get your trees and shrubs in the ground during this phase, too.

Earth signs are good for root crops, so plant onions, potatoes, radishes, and turnips in a Taurus Moon. Transplanting out to the field is also recommended. Taurus falls in the Moon's waxing phase (the planting phase) until about Labor Day, the first Monday in September. Set up a compost heap when Taurus is in the waning Moon, May to either September or October, when Earth energy is pulling downward. Taurus favorably affects compost, because of the Earth and nurturing Venus rulership.

Taurus, ruled by Venus, reigns over the collection of things, and so harvesting, preserving, and storing under a Taurus Moon are favored. Taurus loves to create a beautiful home, with objects in gardens collected to enhance comfort and beauty. Creating a homey abode becomes sweeter with this influence, and so appreciated that one may not want to leave! Good thing because there is always something to collect under a Taurus Moon. From the biodynamic perspective via Maria Thun, Taurus is in the descending phase until late autumn, which brings an extra energetic bonus for storage, especially for root crops.

Gemini ♊ *The Twins*

Keywords: communicative, curious, intelligent
Quality: mutable
Element: Air
Planet: Mercury—delivery of information, fast moving, the winged messenger
Plants: carrots, daffodils, lily of the valley, oats, flowers in general
Herbs: calendula (*Calendula officinalis*), dill (*Anethum graveolens*), lavender (*Lavandula angustifolia*), marjoram (*Origanum majorana*), parsley (*Petroselinum crispum*)
Color: yellow

The astrological Twins are ruled by Air and do not favor planting or transplanting. Flowers are governed by Air, but a Gemini Moon is the exception because Gemini is dry and barren. Instead, this is the time for cultivating, weeding, and mowing lawns to retard growth, combat pests, and prune with limited regrowth, especially in the Last Quarter to New Moon. Harvest fruits and root crops during this phase, banking on the added benefit of the waning Gemini Moon lasting in that harvest from the beginning of summer into late winter.

Gemini rules vascular system (along with arms, hands, and shoulders) and thus melons and celery may do well sown under this influence. In the waning Moon, fertilize with organic phosphorus for flowers. Use rock phosphate for the most economical choice, but keep in mind that it will take four months or more for the soil ecosystem to transform rock phosphate into forms that are available to plants.

Cancer ♋ *The Crab*

Keywords: careful, comfort-seeking, sensitive
Quality: cardinal
Element: Water
Planet: Moon—dreamy, emotional, sensitive
Plants: sap-rich plants
Herbs: aloe (*Aloe vera*), blue vervain (*Verbena hastata*), lemon balm (*Melissa officinalis*), lily (*Lilium* spp.) peppermint (*Mentha piperita*), sage (*Salvia officinalis*), spearmint (*Mentha spicata*)
Color: ice or light blue

Cancer is ruled by the Moon and so represents all things that are motherly, sensitive to others' needs, and feminine. Cancer/Moon is the giver of life-sustaining moisture. Cancer is the cardinal Water sign and brings in summer. Activities that involve watering are favored, and Cancer is the best sign of all for planting. Seeds will germinate quickly. In fact, Cancer is so watery that under a Cancer Moon, lettuce can be sown in the Last Quarter to provide balance so the plants will not bolt to seed too quickly.

Moist and very fruitful, a Cancer Moon is also an excellent time for transplanting and irrigation. Remember to water and fertilize your potted plants during this favorable phase as well, for extra-efficient water uptake.

Cancer is also the most productive sign, ruling lush green leaves and great growth on stalks and vines (not for sturdiness, but lush growth). This would be a very favorable time to sow cover crops. It is also a good time to bud and graft, with those moist Cancer influences at your energetic fingertips.

Cancer is in a waxing Moon phase from winter till summer and in a waning phase from summer to winter, giving you three days of exceptional planting time each month throughout spring until the planting season tapers off in late fall and winter. Harvest and storage activities are not advisable during a Cancer Moon, even in the Last Quarter to New Moon, because it is too watery.

If the Cancer Moon falls on the days after a New Moon, your peas will be productive and have abundant flowers and yield.
Plant peas in Cancer just past a New Moon for quick, abundant flowers and yield.
Peas sown after the First Quarter will bear just a little.
Sown after a Full Moon, they will bloom in abundance but fruit little.

—Louise Riotte

Leo ♌ *The Lion*

Keywords: appreciative, confident, radiant
Quality: fixed
Element: Fire
Planet: Sun—bold, extroverted
Plants: citrus, corn, palm trees, peppers, seeds in general
Herbs: celandine (*Chelidonium majus*), hawthorns (*Crataegus* spp.), marigold (*Tagetes* spp.), motherwort (*Leonurus cardiaca*), sunflower (*Helianthus annuus*)
Color: golden

Leo represents the Sun shining on everything and everyone. Grab some hoes, hand one to a friend, and have a good time eliminating weeds, knowing your actions will be effective and sparked with pleasant conversation and joy, since Leo rules the heart.

This is the most barren and dry sign. Leo is fiery and yang for extra stamina. If you use this sign for weeding, pruning, destroying unwanted growth (including spreading roots and weedy trees), and controlling pests, especially in the Last Quarter, your efforts will be most effective. Mow lawns under this influence to slow growth.

The long sunny days of the Leo Sun bring many plants into flower. Look to harvest your herbs as the vegetative tips develop smaller leaves, just before they flower, to catch the optimal potency for medicine or culinary uses.

Leo rules the heart, so collect and prepare heart medicine with hawthorn or motherwort under this Moon.

Leo is in a waxing Moon phase from around February until August, then shifts to a waning phase from August to February. This tells us that for eliminating weeds or pests, this influence is more dynamic around August till after the freeze in a temperate region. Check your calendars and almanacs for the exact months that this shift happens.

Virgo ♍ *The Virgin*

Keywords: perfection, precise, purity
Quality: mutable
Element: Earth
Planet: Mercury—messenger of beauty and order
Plants: all roots; carrots; nut-bearing trees; small, bright-colored
   flowers in general
Herbs: eucalyptus, fennel (*Foeniculum vulgare*), lavender (*Lavandula angustifolia*), myrtle (*Myrtus* spp.)
Color: brown

Virgo is moist and feminine but barren. After all, she is the virgin, offering beauty and desire but not fruit. Virgo can also be interpreted as the woman who rules her life independently with power and discretion. Therefore, planting and transplanting vegetables are not recommended under a Virgo Moon, especially in the case of fruiting crops, such as tomatoes and peppers. Flowers are favored under this influence of beauty, which would be enhanced by the influence of non-fruitfulness, unless you are growing flowers that have showy seeds, as in the case of sunflowers. Flowering vines can be planted at this time, but not if you wish to harvest fruits from them.

This influence, guided by Mercury, the ultimate messenger, makes it easy to create beauty, easily perceived in the garden or home, in yourself, or anywhere. This Moon is a great influence for potted plants. Have your containers and annuals ready for planting under a Virgo Moon or for potting up or transplanting to a larger pot. Try planting an ornamental vine along one side of your patio if you need a quick windbreak or shade. Remember, though, as it casts shade on you, it will shade your pots of annuals as well!

Try cleaning and organizing your garden shed or home during the time of this tidy and particular influence. (I have tried this and the results were astonishing! Quick and decisive, I was able to clean the garden shed with ease.) Other activities include planting specimen trees and hedges, dividing plants, and setting up compost (in a waning Moon). Do not harvest, store, or preserve under this influence.

Virgo is in a waxing Moon phase from about the spring equinox to the autumnal equinox, with the reverse for the waning Moon phase. This Moon should encourage us all to plant more flowers, food for the soul.

Libra ♎ *The Scales*

Keywords: adaptive, stable, understanding
Quality: cardinal
Element: Air
Planet: Venus—empathetic, fair, orderly
Plants: broccoli, eggplant, juniper, flowers in general
Herbs: cleavers (*Galium aparine*), elderberry (*Sambucus canadensis, S. nigra*), lilac (*Syringa* spp.), mints (*Mentha* spp.), parsley (*Petroselinum crispum*), yarrow (*Achillea millefolium*)
Color: rose pink

Although Libra is an Air sign, it is considered fairly fruitful and moist. After all, the scales represent balance; they provide neutral energy and balance moisture and dryness. That said, we can see why Libra produces pulpy growth, which would be good for grains and other

This row of calendulas ready for harvest looks so luscious it must have been planted during a Libra Moon.

carbohydrate-rich vegetables like legumes, cabbage-family crops, vine crops, and tubers for seed.

Libra, governed by Venus, guides us to seek beauty and requests that our fingertips plant flowers. Remember, flowers are governed by Air, and Libra is the cardinal Air sign, which is considered the best sign to plant flowers.

A Libra Moon is waxing from spring until autumn, favoring aboveground planting, but switches to waning from fall until spring, which is good for below-ground plants, like flower bulbs. While the Libra Moon is waxing, it is a good time to harvest medicinal herbs. And with a waning Libra Moon, process these herbs for creams and salves.

Scorpio ♏ The Scorpion

Keywords: intense, observant, regenerative
Quality: fixed
Element: Water
Planet: Mars, Pluto—evolving, intense, renewing
Plants: bushy trees, leaves of all plants, mushrooms
Herbs: aloe (*Aloe* spp.), basil (*Ocimum* spp.), ginseng (*Panax ginseng*),
   saw palmetto (*Serenoa repens*), wormwood (*Artemisia absinthium*)
Color: dark red

Scorpio is a fixed Water sign, so a good choice for planting, transplanting, and irrigating. In fact, it is the second-best choice for these activities (Cancer is best). But Scorpio has the extra benefit of adding sturdiness, especially for tomatoes and vine crops—think the shell of a scorpion.

As a ruler of the sexual organs, Scorpio benefits fruit production and pollinators. It rules buds and with the effects from Taurus (sturdiness) assists in winter hardiness, even providing a nudge after the sting of winter burn on shrubs and other vulnerable plants. This sign would be helpful for offering winter-burned plants a bit of fertilizer once the danger of frost has passed. A Scorpio Moon is also said to offer protection against early and late frosts. (Remember, never fertilize near a frost time. The lush new growth is most susceptible to frost damage.) Harvesting and working with medicinal herbs is recommended at this time, as well as watering potted plants. But Scorpio's influence is not favorable for harvesting for storage since it is ruled by Water.

In temperate regions, Scorpio is in the waxing phase during the entire growing season, from May to November. In the winter months, Scorpio is found under a waning Moon, so this works in our favor for planting during the waxing phase. Plant corn in a Scorpio Moon, but do not harvest potatoes because they may deteriorate and rot prematurely.

Scorpio is the sign most likely to swing between good and evil, like the scorpion you can't see that suddenly strikes, and the result can become a serious condition for a period of time. *The Old Farmer's Almanac* says to demolish, slaughter, and breed under a Scorpio Moon. Other household tasks include asking for loans, brewing, making pickles, fermenting in general, and canning vegetables. I use the symbol of the scorpion shell to remember to can during this time. Water is what is used to hold canned goods, so can under a Scorpio or Cancer Moon. However, because Scorpio is a fixed Water sign, watch out for mushy pickles and don't leave them in a water bath for too long. An old-timer and pickle expert in Wisconsin, Helen Thibodeau, recommends putting your jarred pickles in a cold-water bath to start. Then bring the water to a boil and remove the jars promptly. She has served crunchy pickles for generations!

Sagittarius ♐ *The Archer*

Keywords: adventurous, expansive, inquisitive
Quality: mutable
Element: Fire
Planet: Jupiter—curious, freethinking, limitless
Plants: ash trees, asparagus, beets, oak trees, rhubarb, tomatoes
Herbs: borage (*Borago officinalis*), clematis (*Clematis* spp.), horsetail (*Equisetum* spp.), hyssop (*Hyssopus officinalis*), jasmine (*Jasminum grandiflorum*), nutmeg (*Myristica fragrans*), sage (*Salvia officinalis*)
Color: purple

This mutable Fire sign is singly pointed, often to fun! It is considered barren and is fiery and yang. Because of its mutable nature, it can lean toward the Earth element, so root crops can be planted under its influence. Aimed upward, like the archer's arrow, Sagittarius is ruled by Fire and is categorized under seed and fruit days. The Moon in Sagittarius can be a good time for planting or pruning fruit trees, since Sagittarius rules fruit.

Harvest fruits and vegetables under a Sagittarius Moon for optimal storage. Cultivate grain for storage and fertilize around or after the Full Moon.

The Fire elements governing Sagittarius are perfect for drying meats, fruits, and vegetables. This sign also favors pruning, with the Moon phases in Sagittarius form working in our favor. The dormant months (the best time for pruning most woody ornamentals) start around the winter solstice and last to the summer solstice.

The archer's arrow also reminds me to go camping or pursue some serious star gazing. Sagittarius is light and its good-natured energy is nice for gathering with friends under the stars or around a campfire.

Capricorn ♑ *The Goat, or Goat-Fish*

Keywords: driven, intellectual, practical, spiritual
Quality: cardinal
Element: Earth
Planet: Saturn—boundary-setting, goal-oriented, structure-based
Plants: beets, parsnips, pines, willows, all roots
Herbs: comfrey (*Symphytum officinale*), onions (*Allium* spp.), rosemary
    (*Rosmarinus officinalis*), rue (*Ruta graveolens*), thyme (*Thymus vulgaris*)
Color: black

In the yearly cycle, this cardinal Earth sign begins on the winter sol-stice. Although it is earthy and yin, it is ruled by rule-declaring Saturn. The combination reminds me of my mother, a beautiful, stern woman who ran a tight ship. Her Capricorn Sun sign is why our house always looked perfect. She scheduled every cleaning task, down to when books on shelves needed to be dusted.

These roots of Solomon's seal were harvested in the Last Quarter under the influence of Moon in Capricorn.

All Earth signs rule roots, so this is a good sign to plant root crops, apply organic fertilizers, and set up a compost bin. It is also a time that benefits tree and shrub planting. Capricorn rules the hormones that affect plant growth and that promote strong apical dominance, for producing strong branches and a symmetrical form for woody landscape plants. Ferment your produce and weed roots with Capricorn in the waning phase.

Capricorn rules the knees and, with the sturdiness of a goat, offers strength for setting posts or pouring concrete. Create garden paths, erect fences, and provide garden structures in this durable phase. Logging is also favored during a Capricorn Moon. The waxing Moon phase in Capricorn is from near July to January: this is the time to cut wood for bending. January to July is the waning phase and favors a building-wood harvest, which would correspond with the time for cutting wood to heat the house (hopefully for the following season, when it will be fully dried).

Aquarius ♒ *The Water Bearer*

Keywords: egalitarian, independent, knowing
Quality: fixed
Element: Air
Planet: Saturn, Uranus—changemaking, creative, revolutionary
Plants: flowers on all plants, most fruit trees
Herbs: cannabis (*Cannabis* spp.), orchids (Orchidaceae family)
Color: turquoise

Aquarius is often thought of as a Water sign, but it is the Water *Bearer*, like clouds moving through the air, bringing moisture for rain or snow. It is mutable, so the essence of Pisces, the next sign in the zodiac, can influence it. Still, it is airy, dry, and yang, and used for cultivation, hoeing, and destroying noxious growths, weeds, and pests. Use this sign to harvest fruit, flower, and root crops. An infertile sign, Aquarius is unfavorable for transplanting but useful for thinning plants.

Aquarius rules the crown of the plant, the point from which top growth emerges upward and roots extend down. The herb Rhodiola comes to mind; with its bulbous nature, it would be a good choice for harvesting under an Aquarius Moon.

An Aquarius Moon is a favorable time for harvesting *Rhodiola rosea*. Photo by Diane Lasceski-Michaels

Pisces ♓ *The Fishes*

Keywords: meditative, sensitive
Quality: mutable
Element: water
Planet: Jupiter, Neptune—deep, dreamy, mystical
Plants: tulips, leaves of all plants, water plants
Herbs: basils (*Ocimum* spp.), lemon balm (*Melissa officinalis*),
    water lilies (Nymphaeaceae family)
Color: sea green

The Water signs are the best for planting, with an affinity for leaf growth. Pisces falls right in line, but because it rules the feet, it produces shorter top growth. Think also of the symbol of the fishes, which dip downward. Dry areas where you need exceptional root growth to source water can be used favorably with this influence. The strong underground growth can take in extra nutrition, which supports a healthy and plentiful fruit crop. Plant vegetables in a waxing Pisces Moon but water and fertilize when waning. This time is unfavorable for pruning fruit trees and shrubs or harvesting for storage due to its watery nature.

There is a bit of controversy about planting potatoes under a Pisces Moon. Although I have been told that it is okay to plant potatoes in the Last Quarter, this could cause misshaping. But in storage, the eyes tend to sprout more.

Jams and jellies can be preserved when the Moon is in a Water sign. I correlate this recommended activity with preserves often stored underground in a root cellar or basement, much like a fish living beneath the soil surface.

And to end on a household note: activities for a Pisces Moon include washing floors and nurturing wavy hair or getting a permanent. (Not at the same time!)

CHAPTER 5

New Moon Gardening Activities

Picture yourself grabbing a seed packet in the early spring. The packet label reads *Calendula officinalis*. You open it; the seeds look like little tan-colored smiles. The moment is full of expectation and wonder. Will the seeds germinate? Will they produce yellow flowers, or orange? Will they grow into something beautiful, worthy of your efforts? Will the weather assist them or curse them? How is it possible for these featherlight seeds to hold all the genetic material that imbues calendulas with their topical healing and antifungal power, complete with a Neptunian glimmer on their petals? This moment depicts the New Moon for gardeners. Like the moment of childbirth, it holds the mystery and wonder of life. It is a dormant time, but you hold seeds in your hand and your soil is ready to receive them.

The New Moon holds the energy of renewal. Also called the dark of the Moon, this inward time offers great potential and energy, but it is difficult to see how things will manifest. We are in a dreamlike stage, returning from the void. I have seen David lie down and rest for hours at the time of the New Moon, even though it's his nature to run around constantly getting things done. It's a remarkable change of behavior for him, and I find it relaxing just to witness him so fully enjoying a brief time of rest.

The word *inspiration* shares a connection with the word *spirit. Inspirare* is Latin for "to breathe or blow into," like a friendly spirit giving you a personalized insight. The New Moon is the time for inspiration,

The New Moon by the Numbers

The New Moon begins the lunar month; it starts at day one and continues for the first week. The New Moon rises and sets with the Sun, shifting 50 minutes later each day after the exact New Moon. Because the New Moon is out during the day, from about six a.m. to six p.m., it can be very difficult to distinguish in the bright daytime sky.

As the New Moon begins, the Moon changes from 0 to 45 degrees of illumination (from our perspective on Earth), with the right half of the Moon's disc growing in light.

The Waxing Crescent arrives three and a half days after the start of the New Moon and lasts to day seven. During the Waxing Crescent, the Moon increases from 45 to 90 degrees of illumination.

for visualizing what you want to create. This period of darkness and inward focus would be a great time for garden design, hearing whispers of distinctive plants that speak to you in the quiet. Bitters, immune support, hormonal balance, liver cleansing—what do you think you need? I believe plants want to support us. Plant them wherever you can, whether it's in a garden or in pots, or if need be, in the garden at a friend's house. This is a mutual love affair waiting to happen!

Someone I know without garden space rogue-planted in open public places or empty lots for a later harvest. This practice became a movement in Detroit and other places, where people would plant vegetable gardens and fruit trees in open, unused ground, with the intention that anyone could harvest their plantings. Urban agriculture or agrihoods are recreating civilizations that connect people and plants for increased health, access to fresh foods, and the common good of all, where neighbors meet over fresh produce. This seems way more sensible than golf courses!

The New Moon is invisible, hidden in shadow between the Earth and the Sun, with its lighted face toward the Sun. Because the Sun and the New Moon are lined up on the same side of the Earth, they move into the same astrological sign at about the same time. Thus, when the Sun moves into the constellation of Aries, it is also a New Moon in Aries. The following month as the Sun enters the constellation of Taurus, the New Moon is in Taurus, too.

Sowing Seeds According to the Moon's Influences

Although the moment of a New Moon holds the mystery of the darkness, it doesn't last long. After all, those seeds are in our hands, the soil is ready.

Did you ever watch a seed germinate, with the radicle or first root initially popping out of the imbibed seed? This is the energy of the Waxing Crescent, which follows the New Moon. The Waxing Crescent is a time of beginnings and has the momentum to get things started. Sowing Seeds for Growth is the slogan during this phase, both in our lives and in our horticultural endeavors.

The energy of the New Moon shifting to waxing is subtler than at the Full Moon.

This time of visualizing outcomes and starting seeds is a perfect match. As you sow your seeds, imagine the beautiful photos of the plant as you have seen it in catalogs or online, or reflect on the potent medicine it contributes and has become known for through the ages.

By sowing seeds, you are taking the unmanifest into a place of fruition—a perfect activity for the New Moon and Waxing Crescent.

Sowing seeds is one of the most important times to pay attention to the Moon's influence, especially when planting seeds directly in the garden. When you are sowing seeds in pots or flats, it is still a matter of debate whether

Keywords for the New Moon

Beginning
Initiating
Expanding
Exploring
Gaining insights

I keep a patch of garden closer to the house for an early crop of greens. Radicchio, lettuce, and fennel. Yum!

the lunar influence is important. My experience tells me that even seeds sown in flats or containers in a greenhouse will feel the magnetic pull from the Moon during this phase and will also be subject to the prevailing zodiacal influence. The energy of the water table is still rising, which would offer an upward momentum.

The best signs for planting are the moist signs of the elements Water and Earth. The Earth signs—Taurus, Virgo, and Capricorn—are especially good for root growth, but are moist and so are still recommended for planting seeds. Virgo is an anomaly and is not recommended for fruiting plants but for beauty. The other planting signs are the Water signs—Cancer, Scorpio, and Pisces—which are recommended for leaves and stems. They are moist signs and are good for planting. Any of these are a good time for strong leaf growth. Leafy crops and grains are especially favored during this first week of the cycle.

More generally, the New Moon favors annuals, plants whose life cycle is completed in one year. They go from seed, to flowering, and back to seed in one year. This New Moon phase is the best time to plant crops that produce their seeds outside the fruit, such as lettuce, grains, spinach, broccoli and other crucifers, flowering annuals, and leafy herbs such as mints and basils.

Cucumbers seem to be an exception to this rule, perhaps because they are so leafy and need lots of moisture to produce. Even though their seeds are inside the fruit, they do well when planted in the First Quarter, the week after the New Moon.

An ancient agricultural practice in Germany calls for planting lettuce only during the waning Moon, perhaps to keep the plant more sturdy and less likely to bolt early. Maybe this is why I have had varied luck with my most frequently planted crop, lettuce. Here in Zone 4, I plant lettuce once a month from March to early September. I sow the September crop in a bed in a greenhouse for the fall and spring harvest. Lettuce seed does not germinate when ambient temperature is over 80°F (27°C), so during the hot months. I sow a flat of seeds in the basement, providing some light because the seeds are light-dependent germinators. My salads are popular at potluck dinners because they are always so fresh and vibrant, and I enjoy them immensely during their seasons.

More Gardening Tips for the New Moon and Waxing Crescent

★ Add lime to the soil in the New Moon or First Quarter, (waxing Moon) by the end of February, in a Fire or Air sign.

★ Repot geraniums.

★ Erect fences, especially in Capricorn.

★ Cut back diseased or weakened plants for rejuvenation. In fact, diseased or damaged plants can recover better when cut back during this rejuvenating time.

★ Prune for more growth. Soil moisture is up, causing plants to swell. Pruning helps this liquid life from the Earth move in the right direction—toward buds held in place until they are triggered to expand. Light, temperature, and day length influence bud break, as well. Pruning helps the favored buds break and timing will increase the flush of growth.

★ Turn the soil for aeration between the New Moon and Full when there is less moisture in the soil. It is lighter and easier to work. This is best done in a barren sign such as Gemini, Leo, or Virgo, and as second best, Aries, Capricorn, and Aquarius.

★ Plant annuals that grow their seeds on the inside of the fruit—such as beans, melons, peas, and tomatoes, particularly if you are growing crops to harvest the seed for either future plantings or edible use.

A Note on Medicinal Herbs

Herbs have archetypes, just like humans, and develop with the same cosmic influences as we do. Open your mind to discover connections to help you to learn how the plants work, how planets influence environments and health, and what a person is lacking or what part needs support. This is one reason I love herbalism so much. It is interactive. You uncover an imbalance your body is communicating to you, and you do research to see what herbs can support that body system. Usually, before long, you'll find that an herb or two keeps popping up, either in your research, or in your life.

Years ago, I noticed a small wart on my finger. I looked up information on plants than can be used to dissolve warts. Then, within a week, a new plant that I did not recognize started spreading in a bed just under my living room window. I keyed it out and learned that it was celandine (*Chelidonium majus*), one of the herbs recommended for treating warts. I tried applying the crushed leaf directly on the wart for a week, and *voila*, it worked like a charm. Having experiences like this builds trust that there is communication and support coming from Nature. Practicing herbalism is interactive, like calling a friend to join you for an activity but the friend is a plant.

Looking to be aligned with larger unseen influences for when to plant, harvest, or make medicine can give you insights into the medicinal messages of herbs, connecting the constituents to the spirit of the plant. We are all made of stardust. Or if that is too esoteric, look at the science showing the paths that connect herbal constituents to the body's physiology. David Hoffmann, British herbalist, phytotherapist, and author of seventeen books on herbs does a great job of blending traditional plant lore with phytochemistry. Also check the American Botanical Council for the science inside these potent healing plants.

To potentize your medicinal herbs, select the day that governs the plant you are working with to properly align with that body system. Say you want to make a brain tonic using ginkgo (*Gingko biloba*), gotu kola (*Centella asiatica*), and rosemary (*Rosmarinus officinalis*). You may choose to make it on a Monday, the day that is associated with the Moon, which governs the brain (as shown in Table 5.1). You can harvest the herbs and/ or make this remedy on a day governed by Aries, which rules the head. Besides utilizing the astrological forces available, you are partnering your intention with the process.

You can select times for your sowing, harvesting, and medicine making according to this system.* The planetary hours developed

---

* You can also find the planets governing the hours of any given day on these two websites: https://www.lunarium.co.uk/planets/hours and https://planetaryhours.net.

Table 5.1 Potentizing Medicinal Herbs

Day	Planet	Inner Being and Energy	Body System
Sunday	**Sun**	the higher self, inspiration	heart, cardiovascular system
Monday	**Moon**	the unconscious, instinct, emotions, emotional connection	stomach, autonomic nervous system, fluids, digestion, brain, lymphatics
Tuesday	**Mars**	vitality, power, action	blood, muscles, reflexes
Wednesday	**Mercury**	the mind, communication, speech, respiration, connection	central nervous system
Thursday	**Jupiter**	hope for the future, joy, expansive, creativity	liver system, thighs, fats/oils
Friday	**Venus**	inner lover, beauty, harmony, comfort, desire	reproductive system, kidneys, thyroid
Saturday	**Saturn**	integrity, structure, foundation, discipline	bones, joints, connective tissue, skin

around 100 BCE, during the Hellenistic astrology era. Starting with the days of the week rulership, planetary days begin at midnight.

The Miracle of Seeds

From childhood, I have been fascinated with seeds. Blowing on the flower stalk of a dandelion took me to a place of wonder as each seed (technically speaking, each fruit) floated on its pappus, or feathery bristles. I watched them artistically dance through the air, and I absorbed and followed the beauty and symmetry of Nature. Dandelion blossoms

Herb	
hawthorns (*Crataegus* spp.) angelica (*Angelica sinensis*) bee balm (*Monarda* spp.)	sunflower (*Helianthus annuus*) St. John's wort (*Hypericum perforatum*)
marshmallow (*Althaea officinalis*) root plantains (*Plantago* spp.) wood betony (*Pedicularis canadensis*)	oat (*Avena sativa*) mugwort (*Artemisia vulgaris*)
arnica (*Arnica montana*) pines (*Pinus* spp.) rehmannia (*Rehmannia glutinosa*) nettles (*Urtica* spp.)	echinaceas (*Echinacea* spp.) chamomile (*Matricaria chamomilla*) yarrow (*Achillea millefolium*)
ginkgo (*Gingko biloba*) gotu kola (*Centella asiatica*) wood betony (*Pedicularis canadensis*)	rosemary (*Rosmarinus officinalis*) mints (*Mentha* spp.) skullcap (*Scutellaria lateriflora*)
dandelion (*Taraxacum officinale*) burdock (*Arctium lappa*) magnolia (*Magnolia officinalis*) bark	American ginseng (*Panax quinquefolius*) rosehips (*Rosa* spp.) borage (*Borago officinalis*)
rose (*Rosa* spp.) petals lemon balm (*Melissa officinalis*) schisandra (*Schisandra chinensis*)	damiana (*Turnera diffusa*) eleuthero (*Eleutherococcus senticosus*) blue vervain (*Verbena hastata*)
comfrey (*Symphytum officinale*) Solomon's seal (*Polygonatum biflorum*) (*Polygonatum* spp.) mullein (*Verbascum thapsus*)	nettles (*Urtica* spp.) horsetails (*Equisetum* spp.) oaks (*Quercus* spp.) teasels (*Dipsacus* spp.)

excited me enough to pick a bouquet for my mother. I might have been five years old, and I remember she did not find those flowers sophisticated enough for her taste. But I was charmed, and I still love dandelions.

I also find spring enchanting, perhaps because I live where the ground is frozen and (hopefully) covered with snow for months. When the first warm weeks present themselves, the spring ephemerals emerge with their short-lived beauty. In this season of my birth and starting seeds, pure excitement bubbles within. After so many years of this ritual, it feels like greeting familiar faces as I identify the seeds of the plants I want to grow. Their shapes and colors are enchanting, from the crumpled texture of round nasturtium (*Tropaeolum majus*) seeds to the tiny seeds of tobacco (*Nicotiana* spp.), no larger than specks of black pepper coming out of a shaker.

From my vantage point as a farmer, I wonder whether those who don't work with plants understand the magnificence of seeds. I am in awe when I pull out my box of seeds in January and realize how they will turn into jars and even freezers full of produce, thousands of pots of tea, herbs that support every body system, a multitude of vases of flowers, and more. How amazing is it that a simple tomato seed holds the potential, when properly placed and cared for, to create vitamin- and flavonoid-rich fruit, full of life-sustaining compounds and complete with next year's seeds! Each seed has a unique shape, color, and texture. They are humble but mighty. We must demand an end to GMO seeds to keep this circle of life intact.

Seeds are amazing, but they come from Nature with no promotional plan to grab your attention. (I am happy that seed catalogs do this for them.) It is easy to be in awe of our phone/camera/mailbox/banking/music/podcast gadgets, but a seed holds enough data to humble an iPhone. When I cradle a seed in my hand, I marvel at all the information stored inside—complex adaptations developed over millennia to survive challenges posed by climatic conditions, soil, pests, and diseases, and more. For many seeds, releasing the potential of all the wisdom gained for thousands of years is as easy as settling the seed in the right seed-starting medium or soil, usually in warm temperatures, and adding water and light (or darkness if that's what the species requires), and it sprouts!

It's a frightening statistic that 93 percent of seed diversity has been lost in the last 100 years. Much of the loss is due to choices made by large seed companies to condense their variety offerings, narrowing diversity to a thin band of genetic material. Fortunately, small companies and home seed savers are working to conserve and promote open-pollinated and traditional varieties.

I do consider hybrid varieties to be a good choice in some cases, especially for disease resistance. Hybrids are simply the progeny of two different parent varieties. After all, people always have wanted to play with plants, and this cross-pollination is sex in action. Traditional hybrid breeding is different from the production of GMOs (genetically modified organisms, whose genes have been altered in a lab and are often marketed by companies with questionable integrity). If you want to know more about the harmful effects of production and use of GMO varieties, I recommend the writings of Indian environmentalist and activist Vandana Shiva. This is a case where we were sold a lie, that this system could reduce starvation, while the numbers of underfed and underserved people continue to grow. According to the Food Tank, a nonprofit devoted to resolving food insecurity, "In 2022, 735 million people—more than 9 percent of the global population—faced chronic undernourishment. Nearly 3 in every 10 people worldwide face moderate or severe food insecurity. Last year was the 10th straight year that hunger levels increased in Africa. Compared to 2019 pre-Covid levels, 122 million more people went hungry last year." These robber baron companies pollute, change laws for their benefit, and limit what seeds are available for farmers to grow. In my area of rural Wisconsin, one farmer had to drive two hours to a seed supply store, passing dozens of others, to get non-GMO corn seed. This sad story has developed over the past twenty years.

The Pleasures and Advantages of Seed-Starting

Why would you bother to start sowing seeds indoors in February or March when transplants can easily be purchased at garden centers in May?

First and foremost, you will experience the thrill of watching seeds germinate, the first tiny seedlings poking up through the growing mix.

In terms of plant choice, the sky is the limit when you order seeds from seed companies. Specialty catalogs offer an expansive choice for almost any kind of plant: annual flowers, perennials, medicinal herbs, vegetables. You might even enjoy the challenge of starting seeds of woody plants.

When you start with seeds, you also have a much wider choice in the color, shape, and flavor of the species that you want to grow. And if you want to grow hard-to-find herbs or perennials, you will have a broader range of selections from seed catalogs. (Here's a tip—if you don't have time or space to start all your plants from seed, shop for plants at a local farmers market. You can often find a good selection of started plants there.)

The plants you grow from purchased seeds will be true to type—most of the time. Most seed houses are reliable in their labelling of the seeds they sell, but every once in a while, I have seen weird mistakes from purchased seeds.

You can time your planting work for days when the Moon is under the correct influence to maximize a successful growing season. You can even fine-tune your desired outcome for a specific use by planting under the appropriate sign that governs that body system.

You can maintain control over the quality of your plants as they grow, and you can make sure they are watered as often as needed and never suffer nutrient deficiency. Transplants at a retail store often aren't watered in a timely fashion, which causes cell structure to break down and the plants may lose leaves. If the plants are left too long in small six-packs or pots, they develop very tight root balls that won't adjust well after transplanting. Plants that have suffered such stresses have a much harder time maximizing their genetics, even if you give them good care after transplanting.

Another tip: If you do buy transplants and discover they have tight root balls, you may be able to encourage more robust growth of

This flat of tulsi germinated in only five days when planted under the influence of a Cancer Moon. It made my eyes pop! (Tulsi usually takes about six days to germinate.)

new roots by cutting off the bottom portion or tearing a piece off of the tight area of the root ball just before you set the transplants into a garden bed.

You will learn more about and feel greater kinship with plants that you grow from seed. As dedicated seedsman Richo Cech of Strictly Medicinal Seeds says, "Grow it to know it."

Getting Ready for Seed Starting

My first step in the growing season is to take inventory of the seeds I have left over from previous years. A digital spreadsheet works well for this task because you can add new columns or tabs for each new year.

Keeping Seeds Organized

If you store seeds from one year to the next, keep them in a cool, dark place with low humidity. Warmth, light, and humidity can ruin viable seeds. I keep seed packets in a tightly sealed plastic bin in the coolest part of a dark basement. I separate them into groups: herbs, vegetables, root crops, and flowers.

Because I have been saving my own seeds for many years, I find it worthwhile to buy 2 × 4-inch (5 × 10 cm) manila envelopes to store them in. Being one of the ultimate recyclers, it took me a long time to give up my penchant to store seeds in any random envelope at hand, but the uniformly sized packets are much tidier and easier to organize.

Once I've reviewed my inventory and made a list of what I need to buy, I order seeds as soon after January first as I can, to ensure my favorites will still be in stock.

It's a good idea to gather your seed-starting supplies in advance. You will need:

- ⋆ seeds
- ⋆ shallow flats/trays and 2- to 4-inch (5–10 cm) pots
- ⋆ covers such as a clear plastic dome or plastic bag to hold in humidity over the tray
- ⋆ watering can or hose end with mist/ breaker nozzle
- ⋆ vermiculite or other light soil medium
- ⋆ labels (a good trick is to cut Venetian blinds into appropriate sizes)

Generally speaking, you'll want to be ready to start seeds six to eight weeks before outdoor planting time. Here in Zone 4, I start the earliest seeds around Valentine's Day. These are crops that take longer to germinate and grow, as well as those that can be transplanted outdoors very early when it still may freeze or frost. Plants in this category are perennials, parsley, and onions.

Crucifers, like broccoli and cabbage, can be sown a couple of weeks later, about March first. When I calculate seed-starting times and expected transplanting dates, I factor in a period of hardening off before transplanting, as I explain later in this chapter.

Since I mainly grow transplants for my own use, not for sale in nurseries, I do not need to produce showy transplants; I concentrate on producing sturdy plants!

Why I Like Vermiculite

You may be surprised to learn that I sow seeds in medium or large vermiculite, not into a seed-starting medium. (I do put a ½ inch [13 mm] deep layer of soil mix on the bottom of each container or flat to hold necessary moisture, and then straight vermiculite on top of that.) I choose vermiculite because plants need air in order to grow healthy roots. Remember, roots grow in the air spaces between soil particles. Bog plants are a different story; they are adapted to mucky soils and dense conditions. But most vegetables, herbs, and flowers need air in the soil! Novices believe seeds and young plants need water, water, water, but air is what generates root hairs and a healthier root system. Experience will show you how to grow plants in the right state of balance between air and water in the soil. Some seeds like it drier than others.

Experience is worth a lot when it comes to growing plants, but even experienced growers learn more every year.

It is also important to use a "sterile medium" to germinate seeds in containers indoors. When I say sterile, I do not mean absolutely void of any living organism. I mean that the medium must be free of plant pathogens and weed seeds. Outdoors in healthy soil, there is a balance between pathogens and beneficial microbes, which creates a favorable environment for the root growth of new seedlings. Wonderful research by Stephen Harrod Buhner proves how this symphony of life below the

Ephedra sown in vermiculite has germinated strongly, and the seedlings will be easy to lift and the roots will untangle easily when it's time to transplant them.

ground surface functions, including communication between plants. I recommend Buhner's writings for more on this topic.

That amazing balance between pests and beneficials cannot be maintained in small pots, however. If you try to put garden soil into pots and sow seeds there, the results will be ruinous. Pathogens will likely take over, causing the roots to rot, or insects pests may hatch from eggs and infest the seedlings and they will fail to thrive. If weed seeds are present, they may germinate faster than your desired plants and shade or crowd them out. Thus, I recommend buying bagged light potting soil or plain vermiculite for starting seeds.

If you are adamant about experimenting with garden soil for starting seeds in containers, you will need to sterilize it first. Place moist soil in a pan no more than 4 inches (10 cm) deep and cover the pan with foil. Make a hole in the foil that you can stick a kitchen thermometer through. Set your oven at approximately 180°F (82°C). Monitor the temperature of the soil. Once it is up to 180°F, hold it at that temperature for 30 minutes. Do not let the soil temperature rise above 180°F, or chemical imbalances can occur that will lead to future crop failure. After the soil has been heated long enough, remove the pan from the oven. Keep foil on to hold moisture in. Allow the soil to cool thoroughly before use.

Another reason vermiculite or sterile mix works well for seed starting is that emerging seedlings don't need any external source of nutrients until after their first true leaves appear. That's because seedlings come equipped with cotyledons, or "seed leaves," that are rich in carbohydrates. These first "leaves" are usually easy to distinguish because they are shaped differently from the typical leaves of the species you are sowing (cotyledons are usually oval-shaped). As the seedling begins to grow, it can use the energy supply from the cotyledons to power growth. Once true leaves form, a plant begins to create energy through photosynthesis, and this is when they will need a supply of nutrients for growth. This is when I apply liquid fish emulsion; weekly is not too much for transplants.

Remember the Labels

It's a helpful practice to label all plants and flats as you sow your seeds. You can fill out labels ahead of time and bring the labels and seed packets to the planting site on planting day. Writing labels is a great time to practice Latin names.

Include the plant name and the planting date on each label. I also like to specify the Moon phase at the time of planting along with the zodiac symbol to indicate the Moon's influence. Here's an example:

Echinacea purpurea, 10 Feb 2020, O, ♈

The O indicates the Full Moon, and the ram's horn symbol is the sign for Aries.

Step-by-Step Seed Starting

Seed starting is a multistage process. You begin by preparing seed flats or trays and sowing the seeds. After the seeds germinate and seedlings are big enough, the next stage is to transplant the seedlings into containers. You'll tend those small plants until they are about to outgrow the pot, at which point you may need to "pot them on" into larger containers or into the garden or field. You will know the plant needs more space when the roots start growing through the bottom of the pot or begin to get tight in the container.

Preparing Seed Flats/Trays

Step 1. Water your soil medium or vermiculite and mix well to ensure it is thoroughly moistened.

Step 2. Pour medium into a flat or tray (be sure they have holes to allow drainage), filling to ½ to 1 inch (13–25 mm) below the top lip of the container. This gap will help to catch water and ensure complete watering of seeds.

Step 3. Tap the surface of the medium gently throughout the container but avoid pressing too hard. This is just to eliminate air pockets or clumps of soil.

Step 4. Make shallow furrows in the medium with a pencil or knife. Typically seeds should be covered only to a depth of twice their diameter, so keep furrows shallow! Using a pencil or knife will keep the furrows narrow, making them easy to cover later.

Time for Seeding

For small-seeded crops, it's best to start by sowing seeds into flats or trays. With larger seeds such as cucumbers, you can plant the seeds directly into small pots or cells, which allows you to skip the transplanting stage. Note also that seeds of some crops, such as dill and cilantro (coriander), prefer to be sown directly into the garden bed.

Step 1. Read seed packet or catalog information to see whether a species has special treatment requirements for germination, such as stratification (a cold treatment) or scarification (nicking the tough seed coat to allow water in). Some seeds require light and others dark to germinate. Some are not specific to either condition. Be sure you provide the treatment, if needed, before sowing or your efforts will be for naught.

Step 2. Cut open the packet and gently tap seeds into the furrow, leaving a ¼ to ½ inch (6–13 mm) between seeds, depending on their diameter, so they will be able to emerge freely from the soil. If the seeds land too close together, gently move them apart with your pencil or knife (rather than a finger) to keep the furrow tidy to receive the seeds. Another technique is to mix very small seeds with sand before sowing; this helps to spread them apart.

Step 3. Cover seeds with ⅛ to ¼ inch (3-6 mm) of soil mix, just enough to hold them in place and keep moisture surrounding the seed. Very tiny seeds, such as tobacco (*Nicotiana* spp.), do not need to be covered at all, and in fact may need to be placed on a finer mix, such as medium or fine vermiculite, so they don't wash down too deeply into the mix when you water them. Some seeds need light to germinate, like lettuce, and do not like to be covered at all. The advantage of a little potting mix over the seeds is that it keeps the vermiculite more evenly moist, an advantage to an imbibing and germinating seed.

Step 4. Water thoroughly but gently, so the seeds stay put. To maintain high humidity, cover the flat/tray with a plastic dome cover or slip it inside a clear plastic bag, leaving one end of the bag open to allow airflow.

Step 5. Place the seed tray in a warm spot. Heat mats are best but try to find a spot that is 65 to 70°F (18–21°C). Putting trays on top of a refrigerator can work well because refrigerators release heat to the outside as they cool their interior contents.

Step 6. Be sure to notice the seedlings as they emerge and move the containers under lights or to a brightly lit spot.

Transplanting Seedlings into Pots

As described earlier in the chapter, the cotyledons unfold first after seedlings emerge from the medium. When the first true leaves appear, it is time to transplant seedlings into individual pots. Fast-growing seedlings like basils can be transplanted directly to the field after growing in flats for six to eight weeks (see chapter 6 for transplanting).

Step 1. Water the seedlings well before you begin the transplanting process.

Step 2. Fill pots with soil mix and place them in a flat that holds water to keep your watering in place (and not dripping on your countertop). You can omit this step in a greenhouse that has drainage.

Step 3. Water the pots to make sure the soil is moist. Gently tap the soil surface to make sure pots are full.

Step 4. Water the pots again and then use a marker pen or dibble stick (a tool used to create a hole in soil) to poke a hole in the soil of each pot. The hole should be big enough to accommodate the roots of a seedling.

Step 5. Gently lift the seedling out of the flat/tray using a knife, spoon, or a widger (a scooped greenhouse tool used to lift seedlings), trying to keep all the roots intact. A short butter knife works almost as well. Gently loosen the soil around the newly formed root to lift it out without damaging the plant.

Step 6. Gently lower the roots of the seedling into one of the pots. Be careful not to "J-root" them, because bent roots must work extra hard to orient themselves to grow downward. These seedlings are your babies, and you want to give them an easy start. Cover the roots with soil, but do not push on the soil, because that would compact it and deprive the roots of air. Water seedlings in their new pots.

Step 7. Place them out of the direct Sun until they are thoroughly established in the pots. Grow lights and bright windowsills are fine. Watch to make sure the stems don't become leggy (stretched out); this is an indication that plants aren't receiving enough light.

Newly transplanted seedlings are a bit unpredictable for watering, do not let them wilt, but do not overwater! See the discussion of this in the next section.

When the plants show their first leaves, they are ready for some organic fertilizer. Follow the directions on the fertilizer package. Young plants can be fertilized weekly in this early phase of the growing season. There are several choices of organic fertilizers for potted plants; I use fish emulsion.

Plants are ready to be transplanted either to the garden or into bigger pots when the roots show through the bottom of the container. If the root ball gets too tight within the pot, it can stunt the plant's growth. If you need to transfer a potted seedling to a larger pot, use a 2- to 4-inch (5–10 cm) pot, or whatever size allows more space for roots to grow, but not too large. Too large makes it more difficult to manage the watering properly.

When transplanting a plant that is root bound, loosen up the roots or even cut off the bottom portion of the root ball to encourage new, free root growth that can follow the force of gravity rather than continuing the pattern of circling the pot's rigid sides.

When and How to Water

Watering plants in pots is a balancing act. You are trying to grow a good root system as much as healthy-looking tops, so maintaining soil aeration is as important as watering when necessary. My favorite way to tell if a potted plant needs water is to lift up the pot and feel whether it is light or heavy. Then you don't have to poke into the soil and disrupt the roots. Most transplants suffer from overwatering. Too much moisture in pots causes weak root growth and increases the habitat for fungus gnats and other pests and pathogens that feed off weak roots.

If you have the time to check your seedlings several times a day, it helps to keep them on the dry side to encourage root growth. I cannot overstate how important it is to not overwater transplants. Drier soil encourages healthy root growth and root hairs, therefore, a healthier plant. Of course, if you know you won't be around during the day to catch them at this point, it can make sense to keep them moister. Every time you water, make sure the soil is completely saturated, penetrating to and through the bottom of the pot. Watch them drip to ensure you watered them completely.

Harden Off!

Before plants started in a greenhouse or under indoor lights are transplanted to the field, they need to be hardened off. "Hardening off" is a technique of placing tender, young potted plants outdoors in a protected spot for a few days, which helps to strengthen their stems and

We grow thousands of medicinal herbs, along with some flower and vegetable transplants, in this well-used greenhouse each spring. These plants fill our production fields plus gardens all over Wisconsin. Photo by Diane Lasceski-Michaels

toughen them up in preparation for the full Sun and wind conditions of the garden or production field. If you skip the hardening off period, your tender plants may not do well at all when you transplant them outdoors.

It is startling to see how potted plants respond to exposure to extra light and wind! Hardening off thickens a plant's cuticle so it can withstand the elements and will lose less water through transpiration. Within two days of being moved outdoors, their tender stems will be turgid and tougher, better able to withstand the jostling of transplanting and wind and from the change of overall conditions. This helps to reduce transplant shock so the plant can make a smooth transition to the field. Ideally, harden off plants for a full week, but if that's not possible, even two to three days will make a difference.

Here are some tips for hardening off young plants.

* Once the plants are the desired size for transplanting, place them outdoors in a protected spot, like under a tree or next to a

building where they will not receive full Sun and wind exposure. On the first day, wait until afternoon to put the plants out, so they have only a few hours' exposure to bright sunlight. If it gets too cold at night, plan on bringing them back in. Unless it is cold-hardy, a baby baby plant resents a night when temperatures dip into the 40s.

* Placing the pots on a wagon or wheelbarrow makes it easier to move the plants in and out in case of nighttime frosts or severe weather.
* After about two days, you can move the plants into increased sunshine and wind.
* Be careful with watering. Plants in small pots need more water out in the wind and Sun than they would indoors, and you don't want to eliminate all the progress you and the plants have gained by allowing them to wilt at this point.
* Ideally, transplant on a still, cloudy day to reduce transplant shock. It is a lucky break if you are gifted these conditions!

I pick up the subject of transplanting in the next chapter, as we turn to gardening activities for the First Quarter.

CHAPTER 6

First Quarter Gardening Activities

We have moved past the New Moon and Waxing Crescent Moon. Your transplants are ready for the field. Remember those calendula seeds you sowed in a flat? When you go out to your garden, you may discover that calendula has already self-sown there. It pays to learn to identify calendula seedlings, so you don't accidentally weed them out by mistake. If you are like me, and love collecting these sun-shiny flowers of softness for salves or need a spark of orange as bright as neon, grow some transplants for an early harvest and save those self-sown seedlings from the garden for your second round of a crop.

The Moon continues expanding from the First Quarter until the Full Moon, bringing its pulsating force to all life on Earth. This energy can be used to move projects outward. The water table is lowered during the day the First Quarter begins, but from there it rises until it is at its highest with the Full Moon, one week later. The upward movement of soil moisture helps plants to grow and expand.

This period of increasing moisture is a great time for transplants to establish themselves in garden beds or a production field. Organic nitrogen fertilizers that were applied two weeks ago during the previous Last Quarter moon (see chapter 8) should be assimilated into the soil ecosystem by now, with their nutrients available for your transplants.

The First Quarter Moon by the Numbers

The First Quarter spans days seven to ten and a half from the start of the lunar month. It rises around noon and sets around midnight, showing its beauty as the Sun sets, an excellent display from our vantage point on Earth.

The Moon is now one quarter of the way through its monthly journey, and we can see half of the illuminated face. Thus, we call it a half Moon, but the illuminated portion we can see is really only one quarter of the Moon's complete spherical surface. The "dark half" from our view is also only one quarter of the sphere. (You can never see all 360 degrees of the Moon's surface at once.) We see the illuminated portion of the Moon's face filling from 90 to 135 degrees.

The light of the Waxing Gibbous spans days ten and a half to fifteen from the start of the lunar month and increases from 135 to 180 degrees of illumination.

Transplanting

After you harden off your plants (chapter 5), plan an afternoon or evening for transplanting them into the garden, when the Sun is lower in the sky. This means there will be less evaporation from plant surfaces as well as cooler temperatures at night, both of which help alleviate the stress of transplanting. Avoiding transplant shock can make a big difference in plant growth and fruitfulness overall.

Always water in transplants directly, even when rain is predicted. You never know for sure how the clouds will blow and whether or how much rain will hit your beds or fields. Even 2 inches (5 cm) of predicted rain could end up being only enough to moisten the surface of the soil. I speak from experience, having made this mistake! Watering in transplants immediately not only provides a drink to help plants avoid entering shock, it moves soil particles into place all around the root balls, eliminating large air spaces that could dry out the plants.

Sometimes even though you carefully cover the plant's roots with soil (without pushing too hard), there could be an unseen air pocket that you missed when covering the plant, or made by a pesky groundhog or mole, that invisibly causes your plant to dry out.

Planting by the correct Moon phase and sign is most important at seed-sowing time, but I still try to match transplanting times with these influences. The best times to transplant are similar to the best times for seed planting. Transplanting is favored in the New Moon or First Quarter phases for leafy crops, in a Water or Earth sign; and in the Last Quarter for roots in Capricorn, Taurus, or Virgo. To extend your selection of dates, transplant flowers in the Air signs, Gemini, Libra, and Aquarius, and fruits or crops for seeds in a Fire sign, Aries, Leo, or Sagittarius.

You can integrate more information and options by accounting for the ascending and descending Moon. Transplanting time is with the descending Moon, passing through the sign of Cancer and on through Scorpio. As the Moon's path turns southward, the Earth breathes in, flowing energy downward into the root zone. This movement benefits roots, with energy shifting downwards. I imagine it as an energetic tug on the plant, helping to settle it in. This stimulates stronger root growth and lessens the shock from transplanting. This time of the descending Moon is good for planting bulbs and roots as well as for transplanting.

As the Moon turns in Scorpio and begins ascending, the Earth breathes out again, moving energy upward. This is the time for taking cuttings and harvesting for storage, moving energy from the earth via the roots upward. Seeds

Young Sylvie holds an incredible head of broccoli grown from a healthy young transplant that was planted at the ideal time for aboveground crops: the First Quarter.

> ## Keywords for the First Quarter
>
> Perfecting
> Developing
> Overcoming obstacles

are more particular to the element or sign in which they are sown, and timing is not determined by the ascending or descending Moon. This matches *The Old Farmer's Almanac* to the biodynamic principle: one should choose root, or Earth-influenced, signs (Taurus, Virgo, Capricorn) or the Water signs (specifically Cancer, Pisces, or Scorpio) for transplanting.

Vegetative Propagation

Some gardeners successively repot flowering plants into larger and larger pots. This can make for an unsightly and unwieldy potted plant that no longer serves its purpose as a tidy ornamental. Instead, take cuttings!

Propagating plants from cuttings is one of my favorite horticultural activities. It is so satisfying watching the roots sprout from a cutting, keeping it pure to the parent plant's genetics. It's actually a type of cloning. Being able to clone plants through cuttings is especially important with plants that do not produce viable seeds, or whose seeds have a weak germination rate. You can take cuttings from a section of a plant that has become variegated, has a taller or shorter stature, or has any other special characteristic. Cuttings provide a way to increase your numbers of a plant, starting with just one plant, providing it has produced the right type of growth (juvenile growth, as I explain below).

Rejuvenating a plant by taking cuttings improves the ornamental quality and stamina of the plant. After a season of growth, the clone often will be "prettier" than the more woody and irregularly shaped mother plant. Plus, a good trick to avoid having plants succumb to pests is to renew them by taking cuttings and then simply getting rid of the older plant. I find this advice impossible to follow for a couple of favorite plants, like potted citrus and bay laurel. I have one of each

104

Want to try vegetative propagation? Try taking cuttings of mint for surefire success. One plant can eventually become an entire field.

of these plants that are forty years old, and I keep them even though they are infested with scale. During long phone conversations, I can use a toothbrush and soapy water to wash off the pests, but the plants are never pest free. Putting these plants outdoors in the summer does wonders because beneficial insects remove many of the sucking pest insects, while new, lush growth covers the scars.

Taking cuttings involves cutting sections of new growth, sticking the cut ends into a rooting medium, and placing them in a favorable environment for the cut-stem ends to develop new roots. Taking cuttings can increase the numbers of your specimen for growing out in the field, selling, or giving away to friends and as party favors. I have given many of my daughter's friends African violets, *Saintpaulia ionantha*, as thank-you gifts for joining us at birthday parties over the years. They were enchanted with having their very own flowering potted plant to grace their windowsills at home.

Some plants evolved to produce their own structures for vegetative reproduction, such as runners on strawberries and eyes on potatoes. Other plants require our skill, tools, and patience for propagation. As a medicinal herb grower, I take cuttings of many kinds of herbaceous perennial plants. Propagation of woody plants is trickier. Woody cuttings can take months to root, so the conditions must be right to keep the cells alive and promote cell growth in the rooting zone.

Cuttings are not for plants in the grass family. They can be multiplied by division—breaking a clump of grass into several rooted pieces—and that's a different process from rooting cuttings. (I describe more about plant division in chapter 8).

The Earth element rules roots. The Earth signs are Taurus, Virgo, and Capricorn; therefore, the energy for root development is enhanced when the Moon is in these astrological signs.

The Sun governs the development of plant shoots and upward growth. The Moon governs roots, round bulbs, tubers, and corms. According to Ernest Michael Kranich, author of *Planetary Influences Upon Plants*, the Moon holds down stoloniferous and rhizomatous plants, like lily of the valley (*Convallaria majalis*), keeping them growing horizontally under the soil surface.

Getting Ready for Taking Cuttings

A month or two before you plan on taking cuttings, start to feed your plant with an organic fertilizer that is relatively high in nitrogen (during the Last Quarter). I like to use bat guano, worm castings, or liquid fish emulsion. Follow the directions on the package and do not overdo it! It is easy to think "more is more" here, but it is also easy to burn roots and foliage tips by applying too much nitrogen. After the new growth has emerged, wait for it to reach the proper stage before taking cuttings.

Plant growth can be classified as embryonic, juvenile, and mature. The embryonic stage is the newly emerged shoot, which is very weak, without a sturdy stem. You can twist and turn an embryonic stem in your fingers without breaking it—it is supple.

The juvenile stage comes next, and this is the stage that will root the best as cuttings. If you inspect a plant closely, you can identify this intermediate growth phase. A juvenile stem has developed enough to feel sturdy, but it still can be bent without breaking, typically. At this stage of growth, the outer layer of tissue has developed enough strength to hold up the plant, but the interior cells are still dividing quickly and have the capacity to differentiate into root growth. This section also has a higher concentration of plant hormones that stimulate root growth, unlike the older sections of the plant. The mature stage often becomes woody or very tough and rigid, unable to produce roots.

Most plant growth occurs around the Full Moon. It's recommended to stick or set cuttings just after the Full Moon. For plants that are more difficult to persuade to form roots—like trees, shrubs, and some vines—take and stick the cuttings (in the rooting media)

More Gardening Tips for the First Quarter and Waxing Gibbous

* Plant vegetables that produce their seeds inside the fruit, such as tomatoes, peppers, beans, and vine crops.
* Sow aboveground crops. In general, the entire two-week period from the New Moon until the Full Moon is good for these crops. Rules regarding aboveground crops are not as hard and fast as some other influences, so both these weeks before the Full Moon work to benefit leafy annuals and other aboveground crops. According to author and gardener Louise Riotte in *Astrological Gardening*: "Many plants, such as melons, garlic, hay cereals and grains, seem to do equally well planted in either phase."
* Consider planting beans. I have tested planting beans in two phases of the Moon. Although the plants grew equally well, the beans planted in the First Quarter, near the Full Moon, kept producing beans throughout the summer, outproducing those planted in the New Moon and Last Quarter. This was an observation, not a repeated experiment.
* Turn the soil to prepare for planting in the waxing Moon phase in a barren Air or Fire sign: preferentially Leo, Gemini, and Virgo. The increasing energy makes the soil lighter and easier to handle by tillage or raking into hills.
* Graft fruit trees close to the Full Moon on a fruit day (Fire signs: Aries, Leo, Sagittarius).
* Make or take tonics and teas for strength and energy. The Waxing Moon is gaining and building energy, so this is the time. Use this outrushing intensity to move projects forward.

Best Herbs for Cuttings

Here are some of the plants I take cuttings of every year. Most of these are clones or selections and do not grow well from seed or do not produce seed. They are all multi-branching. A rose geranium (*Pelargonium graveolens*) in a 2-gallon (7.6 L) pot can yield up to fifty cuttings a year.

Scented geraniums (*Pelargonium* spp.)
Lemon verbena (*Aloysia citrodora*)
Rosemary (*Rosmarinus officinalis*)
Specific varieties of mints (*Mentha* spp.)
Bay laurel (*Laurus nobilis*)
Passionflower (*Passiflora incarnata*)

just before the Full Moon to give them a little more push from the planets.

Step-by-Step Vegetative Propagation

Most of us have tried rooting pieces of ivy in a glass of water, and it worked. So, you might assume that placing a cutting in water is a good way to encourage it to form roots. This is not true for most species! Most plants need more air or carbon dioxide for respiration and growth than they can get from water alone. Many plants that grow in water have evolved root systems that can tolerate being submerged in water all the time. They exploited that niche because nothing else can grow there.

Since water alone is not a good medium for rooting, what should you use for rooting cuttings? The best rooting medium for vegetative propagation is a thoroughly combined mixture of two parts perlite to one part peat. These materials tend to be dusty, so handle them with care, to avoid inhaling the dust. In fact, it's best to wet them before handling them, as explained in the section "Soilless Media for Potted Plants," page 110.

Make sure you have healthy mother plants, free of diseases and pests, to take cuttings from. You do not want to propagate diseased plant tissue or habitat where pests are already in residence.

The amount of time it takes cuttings to root varies widely. Artemisia cuttings can root in as little as one to two weeks, for example. At the other extreme, bay tree cuttings are extremely difficult to root; root formation takes several months.

Step 1. Put moist medium into pots or flats, filling to within 1 inch (2.5 cm) of the lip.

Step 2. Wet the medium in the containers again, so that the weight of the water will tamp down the medium.

Step 3. Use a dibble, stick, or marking pen to create a hole in the mix for each cutting.

Step 4. Take cuttings of juvenile growth that are 4 to 6 inches (10–15 cm) long, using a very sharp knife. Sharpness is important! A dull knife will damage the tissues where the cut is made, potentially creating a place for bacteria to enter the stem. Some easy-to-propagate species, like mints, can root on stems shorter than 4 inches (10 cm).

Step 5. Remove all but the three or four leaves closest to the growing tip. This diminishes the surface area from which water evaporates from the cutting, but leaving just enough leaves to carry the cutting through the rooting process. This step is also important to prevent disease. If lower leaves are left in place and end up pressed into the soil, they rot, potentially ruining the cutting, or even spreading rot bacteria through the entire flat of cuttings.

Step 6. Insert a cutting in a hole and gently tap medium around the cutting to hold it in place.

Step 7. Water the cuttings, wetting the medium completely. This will encourage the medium to flow into any gaps around the base of the cutting.

Step 8. Cover the flat with a plastic lid or plastic bag, or place it on a mist bench. The goal is to create an environment as close to 100 percent humidity as possible to decrease desiccation and wilting of plants. A heat source such as a heat mat underneath the flat or pots greatly increases success.

Step 9. Check plants after seven days to see whether root formation has begun. Gently lift out a cutting to see if root growth emerged. Carefully place the plant end back in the media after checking, unless you are ready to pot them all up. If they are easy to root cuttings, like mints, lift the pots out and look at the bottom drainage holes to see if roots are coming out the bottom of the pot.

Step 10. After the plants begin to differentiate growing roots, gradually open the covering to acclimate the plant to the outdoors.

Step 11. When the cuttings have developed a healthy root structure (1 to 2 inches [2.5–5 cm] of root growth) and acclimated to the decreased humidity, pot them in a light soil mix, using pots that are not much bigger than the root balls of the cuttings.

Step 12. Water them and watch your babies grow into full-grown beauties! Some additional organic fertilizer would benefit their development once the roots are established.

Step 13. After the roots have grown and you pot up the plants, keep them indoors for a couple of weeks to establish fully. Then harden them off as you would regular transplants (as described in the "Harden Off!" section of chapter 5), planting them in the garden or field. Plant rooted cuttings of herbaceous plants during a descending Moon and after the Full Moon.

Soilless Media for Potted Plants

Media for growing cuttings and transplants needs to serve three functions: it must hold both water and air, hold and release nutrients, and provide sufficient support to keep plants upright. Soil media for cuttings and potted plants are usually *soilless*—they do not contain any natural garden soil. Common ingredients for soilless media include perlite, peat, coir, vermiculite, and sand.

Perlite is a form of rhyolite, a volcanic glass-like material, that has been heated to a very high temperature. The glass inflates like popcorn popped in a cast-iron pot, creating a white puff. These particles are very light, with plenty of surface area to hold water and nutrients, releasing them slowly. Perlite holds up well in soil mixes. I use perlite in my soil mixes for all these reasons. Note: Be cautious when working with perlite. The dust can damage your lungs if you inhale it. As soon as you open the bag, add water to the perlite right in the bag. Wetting it helps keep the dust down.

Peat is a type of sphagnum moss that grows around boggy areas. Eighty percent of the peat moss used in horticultural products comes from Canada and is sustainably harvested. Peat moss can hold up to twenty times its weight in water. It is a classic base of most soil mixes.

Coir (pronounced COY-er) is a replacement for peat and is made of the fibers found in the space between the hard inner shell and the outer husk of a coconut. It is sterile, holds moisture, and is very rot resistant. It takes lots of energy-intensive processing to get coir to market, so I stick with using peat moss and do not have much experience with this material.

Vermiculite is an expanded mica. It is light and fluffy. Although it stands up initially, it degrades and loses its form. It collapses over time and loses its moisture-holding capacity. It is clean, lightweight (so bags are easy to lift), and holds moisture very well. I like to use vermiculite for germinating seeds. Because seed starting typically takes a few weeks' time at most, the issue of vermiculite losing its structure is not a concern, as it would be in a container holding a potted plant.

Sand is sometimes blended in soil mix (or garden beds) to facilitate drainage. I never use sand. It is heavy to work with and has little surface area, so it does not hold nutrients or water. Although it is used to improve drainage in heavy soils, sand's physics makes it shift to the top of the soil in a garden bed. (The largest soil particle always rises to the top, and sand is larger than silt and clay particles.) Then it washes away, so what was the point of hauling that heavy material to the garden? In good garden soil, compost and organic matter serve the purpose of providing air spaces and moisture-holding capacity.

CHAPTER 7

Full Moon Gardening Activities

Humanity looked in awe upon the beauty and the ever-lasting duration of creation. The exquisite sky flooded with sunlight. The majesty of the dark night lit by the celestial torches as the holy planetary powers trace their paths in the heavens fixed and steady meter—ordering the growth of things with their secret infusion.

—HERMES TRISMEGISTUS

Basket in hand, you step into the garden and approach the calendula. They are in full bloom, practically shouting with brilliant, sparkling yellow and orange. You have already filled your storage bin for the year and can now share this harvest with others. Or perhaps hold a Full Moon ceremony and use it in your floral mandala.

Creating a ceremony at the Full Moon is a way to show appreciation for the Earth and all its gifts. For many years on the summer solstice, people (most of them women) would gather at my farm and collect flowers and place them on the Earth, creating a beautiful, colorful, living mandala of love for the Earth's beauty.

The Full Moon is a time of culmination, with energy at its peak for all living things. From speaking with doctors and nurses, I know that more babies are born and emergency rooms are busier during this Moon phase. Studies have varying results, but speaking to the people on the ground, they see a difference during the Full Moon. All life is pumping with extra potency. Coral species in the Great Barrier Reef send clouds of sperm and eggs skyward only during the Full Moon.* There are dozens or perhaps hundreds more examples, from sea creatures to *Homo sapiens*, that tune their reproduction and lives according to the Moon cycles. Maybe because I have lived in the countryside all my adult life, growing, harvesting, and observing things, I watch and sense the synchronicity that Nature provides. This rhythm is what I am encouraging others to experience. I am a believer!

The arrival of the Full Moon is a potent day that can be used for creative visualizations and meditations. I have been practicing Full Moon meditations since the late 1990s with a worldwide group called the TSG Foundation. We consider the positive attributes of each astrological sign that is aligned with that month's Moon. This offers insights on how we can integrate the best qualities of each astrological sign. I love engaging these powers as the doors open to these positive qualities to integrate into my life, especially on the exact day of the Full Moon. This meditation can be done for five to seven days. You can start two or three days before the Full Moon, continue through the day of the Full Moon and on for the next two or three days to really imprint the message into your soul and psyche. This helps me connect to my inner guidance for a more virtuous society. I encourage you to also meditate on the energy of the quality that each zodiac sign offers at the Full Moon, to enhance positive personality shifts. To check out these Full Moon meditations go to www.tsgfoundation.org/monthly-classes.

> We celebrate full Moon festivals in order to examine ourselves and see how we are unfolding, developing, and blooming. Full Moon festivals are times in which we observe and examine our physical, emotional, and mental life and check our orientations.
> **—Torkom Saraydarian,** *The Wisdom of the Zodiac*

---

* BEC Crew, "The Full Moon Just Triggered One of the Largest Mass Spawning Events of 2016," *Science Alert*, November 24, 2016, https://www.sciencealert.com/the-full-moon-just-triggered-one-of-the-largest-mass-spawning-events-of-2016.

The Full Moon by the Numbers

The Full Moon spans days fifteen to eighteen and a half of the lunar cycle. It rises about six p.m. and sets around six a.m. This timing varies depending on your latitude. (It is near the summer solstice as I write this, and where I live, on the forty-third parallel, the Sun sets around nine p.m. and the Moon rises shortly after that.)

At the time of the Full Moon, the Moon is opposite the Sun from our perspective on Earth. Its illuminated portion changes from 180 to 135 degrees, decreasing from the right side instead of increasing to the left.

The Waning Gibbous spans days eighteen and a half to twenty-two of the lunar cycle, three and a half to seven days after the Full Moon. It is visible to us from late night to early morning, rising around nine p.m. and setting around nine a.m. Illumination changes from 135 to 90 degrees.

Celestial Harvesting

The first thing to do before, during, and after a harvest is to feel a sense of gratitude for what Nature has given. Know you are receiving alchemical gifts specially prepared by eons of fine-tuning that support us on our path. This is no small gift! Just think of how the roots of the much-underappreciated dandelion can support liver health, which in turn can influence every system in the body. (The tops or leafy portion have an affinity for the kidney. I use the whole plant to polish up my liver every few weeks.) In the spirit of harvest, joyfully receive your gifts, instead of thinking of the harvest as taking whatever you want.

This moment inspires me, knowing I am a reflection in the big prism of light, with the plants supporting me from below, influenced by the stars above.

I love the sentiments expressed in this poem by Laura Lynch, my 103-year-old neighbor:

I am just a country girl, and money have I none.
But I have silver in the stars at night and gold in the
    morning Sun.

You can cultivate this feeling of abundant appreciation when studying which astrological influence the Moon is in that day. What element is the Full Moon in now?

Using the elements as a guide, I would hope for my harvest that the Moon was in an Air or Fire sign for its dry influence. Remember, Fire governs seeds and fruits, and Air governs flowers. See what you have around to harvest from those plant parts first. If the Moon is in a Water or Earth sign, consider harvesting roots for the Earth sign and leafy portions or herbs under a Water-influenced Moon.

Approaching harvesttime leads me to ponder the variation that Nature provides. What am I really harvesting? Is it the textures, the aromas, the colors? Is it the scene around me, complete with birds singing in the background and a butterfly landing nearby? Or is it the multitudes of constituents compiled in these glorious packages that Nature has devised to be entirely biodegradable—no bottles or plastic packaging to be thrown away or recycled? David and I know we can credit the produce from our gardens, along with our efforts in growing it, for our good health. We are lucky, but we feel that the good choices we consciously make are an important factor in our health and happiness, too. You can even grow good health in containers on a balcony. Our daughter grows seasonal vegetables in pots outside her city apartment, swapping out lettuce for tomatoes as the season progresses. She tends a container of culinary herbs, and I was amazed she even had a pot of dandelion greens grown from seeds collected from a park for her green smoothies!

Gratitude emerges again. I am grateful for these plants but also for my innate interest and desire to spend my

Keywords for the Full Moon

Harvesting
Assimilating
Reorienting
Gaining awareness

More Gardening Tips for the Full Moon and Waning Gibbous

★ Plant root crops, biennials, perennials, and bulbs. During this third week of the Moon's cycle, as soil moisture is retreating, it favors deep root growth. This includes onions, potatoes, carrots, and beets, as well as all kinds of trees, shrubs, and berry bushes.

★ Propagate plants to encourage root growth. Divide perennials when they are beginning a resting phase. It is also a good time for taking cuttings.

★ Harvest above- and belowground crops when the Moon is in Taurus, an Earth sign that rules the collections of things.

★ Make sauerkraut, jams, and jellies when the Moon is in Pisces.

★ Can or pickle when the Moon is in Pisces or Cancer.

★ Dehydrate in a Fire sign (Aries preferred) as the Moon is waning.

★ Harvest fruits and seeds in the Full Moon to New Moon, in a Fire sign.

★ Collect under a Capricorn Moon, a favorable farm activity, Capricorn rules farms, even though it is an Earth sign; it is moister than the Air or Fire signs.

★ Plant cover crops.

★ Prepare the soil by cultivating it three times on Capricorn days, or in a Fire or Air influence.

★ Plant fall crops to be harvested in spring, such as garlic. The old adages "Plant potatoes on Good Friday" or "Plant potatoes in the dark of the Moon" come from this Moon phase. Easter falls on the first Sunday after the first Full Moon after the spring equinox, so Good Friday is always in this quarter of the cycle.

★ Fertilize with organic fertilizers after the Full Moon up to the Last Quarter. The energy is descending and will help incorporate these nutrients into the roots for fortified plant growth.

The Gift of Traditional Knowledge

When I am curious about whether an herb might be a good choice to support my well-being, I look for its seeds first. Tending an herb from seed to harvest begins my relationship with the storehouse of wisdom contained in each leaf. Through the work of generations of women growing, harvesting, and collecting the seeds of this plant to keep the health of their communities vibrant, this plant now lands in my hands. I am grateful for the chance to be in relationship with this plant.

I also pause for a moment's reflection and grieve both on the diversity of plant material and all the traditional knowledge that has been lost, wiped out by greed. Yet I remind myself of how many plant treasures have not yet been discovered.

Most people don't know that as they walk across a lawn and step on plantain (*Plantago* spp.), they are stepping on an excellent herb with the power to relieve the pain and itching of any kind of insect bite! Plantain was brought to North America by European immigrants due to its efficacy, and the herb quickly followed the colonizers as they traveled through this beautiful land. Indigenous people named plantain "white man's footprint" for this reason.

life learning from Nature, from wonderful teachers, and through books and conferences. I have witnessed plants as effective agents for health throughout my life, addressing most of the health concerns of myself, my family, and open-minded friends. My outlook has evolved from "This works so well, I believe there is an effective herb for every condition," to "It is astounding how quickly the pharmaceutical industry wiped out any sense of trust in Nature's cures." That transformation in attitudes toward herbal medicine has taken place in less than 100 years. My inner knowing and relationship with these plants and my choice to stand by herbs as a source of healing held me up to intense social pressure recently when any deviation from the proclamations of the conventional medical system were considered heresy. My experiment worked. In my experience, elderberry (*Sambucus canadensis*), echinacea or purple coneflower, (*Echinacea angustifolia*), boneset (*Eupatorium perfoliatum*), and andrographis (*Andrographis paniculate*) were as effective as conventional medicine would have been.

Moon and Planetary Influence on Harvesting

Now that you have invested your time and devotion in your plants, the Full Moon is the time to capture the potent constituents that these plants have produced for the benefit of humans and others.

As discussed in chapter 2, the alignment of the Earth between the Sun and Moon at the Full Moon causes tides to rise higher than normal, lifts the level of the water table in the soil, and offers an extra impulse to life. With all this potentized energy, this is a good time to gather herbs to process into tinctures, salves, teas or prepare for storage, or to preserve juicy fruits. There is more moisture in the plants, but consider they are full of sugars, nutrients, and flavor, making them favorable for preservation. Herbs and all life forms are pumped full of vitality at the Full Moon.

I love the beauty and strength of these traditional harvest tools on display at the Aboca Museum (a museum devoted to medicinal plants) in Sansepolcro, Italy.

Even though there is more moisture in leaves, fruits, vegetables, and grains at this time, harvesting during the Full Moon ensures the constituents, vitamins, and minerals are at their peak. The advantage to harvesting during a Full Moon is the peak potency. An argument could also be made for harvesting fruits for drying at the time of the New Moon, however, because there would be less moisture in the fruits then, making them less susceptible to rot.

Experiment with harvesting both ways, noting the

days' influences, and find which works best for your conditions. We have noticed we need to rely on both influences—the Full Moon and the New Moon—to gain more opportunity overall to bring in our harvest.

To add the special touch of the planets while preserving fruits, vegetables, syrups, and fermentation, here are some guidelines:

Preserving. The waning Moon brings the energy of moving inward and is used to our advantage when canning, pickling, fermenting, and drying. The signs recommended for these activities are Pisces or Cancer (or Scorpio). Pisces is the first choice when it falls after the Full Moon. I picture the fish, which lives happily below the water's surface, to remember that one. Cancer and Scorpio have hard outer shells and soft interiors, so that is how I think of those as canning days.

Drying. Aries is the sign for drying, although the other Fire and Air signs are decent next-best choices. Remember, while harvesting at the Full Moon will bring the pulsating energy of vibrant life, the waning Moon calls the energy inward, which is an advantage for drying, too. I aim to harvest during both a Waning Gibbous and Waning Crescent, but there is no way I will forfeit my arnica (*Arnica chamissonis*) flowers during the other two weeks of the month. I have heard from well-respected herbalists that most arnica is adulterated, so the value of my vibrant yellow, short bloom–season crop will not go to waste. During a waxing Moon, we harvest on Fire and Air signs.

Harvesting for storage. In chapter 8, I discuss harvesting crops to store or dry as a Last Quarter garden activity.

Canning. Pisces and Cancer are favorable for canning. Although Scorpio is a fixed Water sign, it is ruled by fiery Mars, so is less watery by nature. Water is what pickles, fruits and preserves are canned in, so I believe that is why Scorpio is not the first choice here. Imagine the hard outer shell of the crab holding liquidy, soft inner contents like those inside canning jars. The fish symbol in Pisces displays life sustained underwater, like the vitamins in jars of preserved fruits and vegetables.

Harvesting flowers. Air signs correspond to flowers, so Air signs when the Moon is waning are ideal for harvesting your calendula (*Calendula officinalis*), chamomile (*Matricaria chamomilla*), or ornamental flowers for drying. Drying requires airflow. The Fire signs are also favorable for drying crops, because the crops hold moisture and the Fire provides extra drying force. Energy in the plant shifts downward after the Full Moon, drawing moisture from the foliage and stems to the roots, making them easier to dry.

Harvesting Herbs or Leaves

The best time of day to harvest herbs, or the leafy portion of vegetable crops such as lettuce and spinach, is after the dew is dry—about ten a.m. here in the Great Lakes states—but before the essential oils have been volatilized in the warming Sun (by noon). Harvest perennials at about 6 inches (15 cm) above the crown so that they have some stem left for regrowth. When harvesting perennials in the autumn, you can leave just enough stems to trap snow and protect the crown, usually 4 to 6 inches (10–15 cm). Another rule of thumb is to harvest the top two-thirds of the plant and leave the bottom third intact.

Annuals can be cut closer to the ground because the plant is completing its lifecycle at harvesttime and we don't expect it to regrow. Of course, with all the care a grower puts into each crop, only the perfect leaves should be harvested, not the blemished or yellowed leaves. At Four Elements Organic Herbals, we cut the stems just above the point where rain has splashed soil up onto the plants. It

Herb-Harvest Timing Tips

The best time to harvest an herb is:

★ After the morning dew is dry but before Sun's heat causes the plant's volatile oils to escape (around late morning).
★ During a Full Moon or Last Quarter, in an Air or Fire sign.
★ Just as they are coming into flower, when the constituents are at their peak.

The second-best time to harvest an herb is when you are there and the plant is there.

is best not to wash herbs before drying, so harvesting only clean plant material makes the most sense. Look closely at the bottom of the plant to see which leaves show signs of trapped soil. Leave that portion in the field as an offering to renew the soil.

If you plan on harvesting an annual crop more than once, you must leave enough stem and nodes intact at the first harvest so that plants will sprout enough vigorous new growth to make a second harvest worthwhile. Annuals we harvest more than once

White sage is being overharvested in the wild. We grow our own plants from seed.

include tulsi (*Ocimum tenuiflorum*), all types of basils (*Ocimum* spp.), and white sage (*Salvia apiana*), which is grown as an annual in Wisconsin. For the first harvest at midseason, we usually remove only one third to one half of the plant's top growth.

Time the leaf harvest as plants switch from the vegetative stage to flowering. Look for differentiation of developing flowers in the shoot tips. As the plant shifts from one stage to the next, its morphology usually changes. A leafy plant may start to form pointier growing tips, for example. That is the best time to harvest foliage, because the plants are at peak potency when they begin to flower, pumping out the maximum medicinal constituents. Then you can plan your upcoming harvest date according to the dry astrological signs governed by Air and Fire, especially during the Full Moon and waning time.

The Flower Harvest

When an herb plant begins to bloom, that is the time to start collecting its flowers. The more frequently you pick the blossoms, the more the plant will bloom, because it will not have to expend energy on making seeds instead. This is the same principle employed in ornamental gardening—deadheading flowers regularly keeps your beauties in bloom. Cutting weekly bouquets of my cheery zinnias (*Zinnia* spp.) keeps them in constant bloom until the first frost.

We pick chamomile, calendula, and arnica flowers twice a week, when in season. And frequent flower harvesting is especially important for herbs that have a short bloom period, such as arnica. Sometimes you must act based on the practicality of harvesting: when you are there, and the plant is there.

Root and Bark Harvest

When the cool weather sets in and the days become shorter, plants are triggered into dormancy. The energy of the plant starts pulling in and withdrawing its energy into the roots. This is the time to harvest bark and roots. In the autumn, harvest bark as the leaves drop, when the constituents are traveling through inner part of the bark, called the phloem. In the spring, harvest bark as the leaves emerge, during or just past the maple syrup season, as the sap rises. Collect the vibrant green part of the inner bark, where the life and dividing cells are active. If the

This crop of tulsi is ready to be cut and dried.

outer bark is thin, there is no need to remove it, as in the case of small branches of cherry (*Prunus* spp.) bark. I find that a vegetable peeler works great for this purpose, and when you harvest cherry bark in the spring or autumn, the aroma of cherries and almonds will delight your senses. If the outer bark is corky, woody, and thick, the inner bark should be stripped out and removed from the corky outer portion, as in the case of white oak (*Quercus alba*) bark. I once harvested white oak bark in March, as the buds began to swell. Of course, it was cold here in Wisconsin that day, so I was wearing thick leather gloves. Despite the gloves, that night the skin of my hands was cracked because the oak bark is so intensely astringent that it pulled moisture out of my hands even through the gloves. I didn't complain—I knew my cracked skin was a sign that I had harvested effective and active material to blend into my herbal combinations, plus I could apply my botanical creams with comfrey or calendula for an easy fix.

Planting During the Waning Moon Phases

Although many types of plants do best when planted before the Full Moon, there are some exceptions. The water table is highest at the Full Moon but then recedes, creating perfect conditions to gently encourage roots to go deep and follow the water table. Because of this, the time of the waning Moon is good for planting root crops, perennials, trees, and shrubs. Onions, beets, carrots, potatoes, and other root crops benefit from planting in the waning phases.

One spring day many years ago, David mentioned to me that he was planning to plant potatoes that day. I knew it was the time of the First Quarter Moon and thus favorable for planting leafy things but not potatoes. I said, "Could you save me 25 percent of those seed potatoes to plant two weeks from now, when the Moon is favorable?" He agreed to the experiment. We both tended our separate plantings of potatoes. When harvest day came for David's potatoes, he was downtrodden, and told me it was a bad potato year: the tubers he found were small and few. I was optimistic, however. When the day to harvest my potato patch came, I brought in large and beautiful potatoes. David was impressed and has been listening to my guidance from the Moon's wisdom more frequently now.

Perennials, Trees, and Shrubs

You cannot hope to raise healthy perennials, trees, or shrubs unless they have healthy root systems. Since the waning phases of the Moon favor root growth, this is the time to plant and transplant this group. Choose a day when the Moon is an Earth sign (Taurus, Virgo, Capricorn); or for nonfruiting trees or shrubs, choose a time when the Moon is in a Water sign (Cancer, Scorpio, Pisces). Because the water table has been high, you will be setting the roots into moist ground, which is important for their early adjustment to the new location. As time passes and the water table recedes, the roots will stretch downward, following the receding water table, as time passes. This is also a favorable time to dig and divide perennials; they will recover quickly from the stress of division.

Laying Down Cover Crops

David has nurtured the most beautiful fields of fertile soil on our farm using organic methods, including cover cropping and careful cultivation. David even installed native prairie plants using organic methods. This was a triumph because, even for a project as life-sustaining as creating a prairie, the standard procedure is to first kill the existing vegetation on the site using glyphosate (such as Roundup), an herbicide shown in multiple research studies to be a cancer-causing agent. Bayer, the company that now manufactures Roundup, has paid out billions of dollars for the purpose of settling nearly 100,000 lawsuits brought against the company by people who developed non-Hodgkin's lymphoma after exposure to Roundup, according to a 2021 report by Reuters.* To my mind, this is one compelling reason to go organic! Another big reason to garden organically is to protect the quality of your soil and everyone's air and water.

Cover cropping is a management practice that benefits the soil, the plants, and the gardener (or farmer). A cover crop can improve soil health, smother weeds, enhance water availability, slow erosion,

---

* Tom Hals and Tina Bellon, "Bayer Reaches $2 Billion Deal over Future Roundup Cancer Claims," *Reuters*, February 3, 2021, https://www.reuters.com/article/us-bayer-glyphosate-idUSKBN2A32MX.

If the weather is right, with the waxing Moon in a water sign, cover crops like these oats can emerge in less than a week.

provide pollinator habitat, and increase biodiversity in your soil. The basic technique is to plant grasses, legumes, or forbs—such as clovers, vetch, buckwheat, oats, or rye—to cover the soil. Eventually, after cutting it to a manageable height, it can be tilled back into the soil to provide organic matter. A cover crop may be allowed to grow for as little as four weeks, or sometimes it may be left in place on a garden bed or field for the entire growing season to rejuvenate the soil and add nutrients while improving soil structure. In fact, certified-organic farms are required to take soil acreage out of production every three to five years to improve it in this way.

David has used repeated plantings of cover crops to convert grassland into a productive field where we can grow herbs. The same sequence will work for converting an area of lawn into a home garden.

Step 1. Mow the area low, close to scalping the soil surface.

Step 2. When the soil is at the correct moisture level, till the area. (See "Determining Moisture Level for Cultivation," page 127.) This can be done with a shovel, turning the sod under (upside down) if the area is small enough. Another option is to cover the soil with a barrier, such as cardboard, for a year to kill the grass.

Step 3. After tilling, some tough roots of perennial weeds will regrow in the next week or two. After these begin to grow, till the area again. The timing for your retill will depend on weather conditions—plants may not regrow much if the soil is dry.

Step 4. Repeat tilling three more times as you see perennial weeds resprouting. Repeated tillage weakens perennial roots. It will also kill off annual weed seedlings that have germinated, which will reduce future weed pressure.

Step 5. After the fifth round of tilling overall, it is time to sow the cover crop seed. If it is summertime, plant buckwheat (*Fagopyrum esculentum*). Buckwheat is a fast-growing crop, completing a life cycle from seed to seed in five or six weeks. It also has broad leaves that grow horizontally. Together, these mean that buckwheat quickly establishes a presence and eliminates any light from reaching the soil, putting weeds at a disadvantage. Virtually nothing else grows in a field of buckwheat. It out-competes everything! The crop can be left to go to seed if you want it to reseed and produce another cover crop immediately afterward, or it can be mowed off. Buckwheat is a tender crop that will crash with even a light frost, and the frosted plants create a kind of blanket over the soil.

Step 6. If you are ready to plant in late summer, with six to eight weeks of warm weather still ahead, you can plant oats (*Avena sativa*). A bonus with oats as a cover crop is that the unripe seeds, known as the *milky stage*, can be harvested for use in nerve-support tonics. Oats collected in the milky stage are the best tonic for a marathon nervous-system event, such as grieving the death of a loved one or other long, difficult situations that tax the nervous system.

    To ensure good germination, we broadcast oat (and other types of cover crop) seeds on the soil surface, according to the rate suggested on the seed package, and very lightly till it in, about ¼ inch (6 mm) deep, if possible. Or you can rake the bed by hand; it's another effective way to increase soil contact with seed, which helps stimulate better germination.

Step 7. When it's time to plant a cover crop to leave in place for the fall and winter, try a blend of winter rye (*Secale cereale*) with hairy vetch (*Vicia villosa*). Do not substitute crown vetch (*Securigera varia*), which can reseed and become weedy. Other legume cover crops, such as crimson clover (*Trifolium incarnatum*), red clover (*T. pratense*), or white clover (*T. repens*)

Determining Moisture Level for Cultivation

Here's how to test whether soil is at the right stage of moisture for digging or tilling:

★ Take a representative handful of soil and squeeze it hard. If it will not hold a ball shape, it is too dry to cultivate.
★ Using your fingers, test to see how easily the ball of soil crumbles—or not. If the soil will not crumble, it is too wet to cultivate. If it crumbles, proceed with cultivation.

If conditions are right, cultivation is best done after the Full Moon and especially during the Last Quarter, in an Air or Fire sign, to reduce weed pressure.

are also excellent, but the high cost of many kinds of legume seeds makes them less practical.

Take care to not allow cover crops to go to seed; otherwise, they may become competition for your future vegetables, flowers, and herbs. You can choose to let a cover crop make seed as part of your management strategy, but be aware that the self-sown second crop will be less uniform because the seed matures and falls at different rates. Mow or till it after its life cycle is completed, and then wait a couple weeks before you plant a crop in that spot. Just after tilling, all the available nitrogen in the soil is taken up by soil microbes as they busily feed on decomposing organic matter and their populations expand.

The best phase for planting cover crops are the Full Moon and Waning Gibbous because most cover crops are legumes and grains, and they produce seeds outside the fruit. Wait to till in cover crops during the Last Quarter, if possible, because the sinking water table will help to ensure that the plants are killed off.

For more information on cover cropping, check the Sustainable Agriculture Research and Education (SARE) website at www.sare.org/resources/cover-crops.

Drying Herbs, Fruits, and Vegetables

Drying is a simple and effective way to store herbs, fruits, and vegetables for winter use. Let's start by learning about the joy of drying herbs for storage; insurance for good health, contained in jars!

Kitchen gardeners are often surprised to learn that many culinary herbs are medicinal herbs, too. The sage we use to flavor our baked squashes and turkey dinners has the botanical name *Salvia officinalis*, which translates as "the official healing herb." *Salvia* means "to heal," and *officinalis* indicates placement in the official pharmacy of the time. Thyme, oregano, basils, and more all help to maintain your well-being.

Collecting Bundles of Bounteous Beauty

To dry quality herbs for culinary use or medicine, all that is needed is a dark, dry place, preferably with ample air circulation. Although kitchens tend to be brightly lit rooms, the top of a refrigerator can serve as a spot for drying herbs. The heat radiating from the appliance will have a dehydrating effect, and the herbs will be in good view, which will remind you to tend to them.

The simplest method of collecting herbs is in paper bags. Head out to your garden with paper bags, a pruner, and a marker pen. Cut the portion of the plant you desire, put the cut stems in a bag, and label it with the plant's scientific name (learning the botanical names is a way of deepening your relationship to plants), the date, and the astrological sign of the day (add the planetary influence of the hour, if you are so inclined), along with the Moon's phase.

Leave the bag open and set it in the warm, dry place you have selected. Shake the bag every day to make sure air is flowing throughout the plant material; this will help prevent mold from developing.

Check the material periodically for dryness. When the leaves fall easily off the stem, they are dry enough. Then push the sides of the bag together and vigorously rub to crunch the leaves off the stems. This is faster than working one stem at a time. After the leaves are off, simply lift the stems out (you can compost them) and pour the dried herb material from the bag into an airtight container. Transfer the information you wrote on the bag onto your storage container.

Store dried herbs in glass jars or tins, lined with paper bags. Containers should not let light in, because exposure to light degrades the color and quality of the herbs. If you use clear glass jars without the paper lining, store them in a cupboard, out of the light.

Avoid storing herbs (or any dried foods) in plastic containers. Plastic containers will not hold the essential oils in the herbs, and herbs stored in plastic will degrade and lose their potency over time. Plus, of course, plastic is one of the worst pollutants we are dealing with at this time on Earth. Microplastics are showing up everywhere: in the oceans, in fish, and even in human placentas. Just say no to plastic.

Sage and chamomile are a beautiful garden combination. Cut them fresh as needed and make bundles for bouquets. Photo by Diane Lasceski-Michaels

Preparing Fruits and Roots for Drying

Fruit and root harvesting require more time and effort than picking leafy stems, but you are collecting the storage unit of the plant, so the potency is concentrated. The reward is worth the work. It's best to collect roots and fruits around the Full Moon if you are going to process them into tinctures or syrups. Collecting in the waning Moon is better if you plan to dry the harvest. Choose a day governed by an Air or Fire sign, unless you are aligning this plant with a remedy for a specific condition, like watery Pisces for a sore foot or Earthy Capricorn for a bum knee.

Fruits and roots contain a lot of moisture and need to be chopped into small pieces so they will dry properly. We use a food processor for chopping, but you can use a sharp knife and cutting board instead if you wish. Cut into ½- to 1-inch (13–25 mm) pieces and spread them on screens to dry. Apples can be peeled and sliced; thread the slices onto strings and hang the strings to dry. Stringing sliced fruits and roots requires more time than chopping, and you must pay careful attention to make sure the fruit does not mold. I have dried carrots, celery (which is a petiole, the botanical part holding the leaf, not a root, but the same process applies because it is moist), apples, pears, raspberries, seedy Concord grapes (which I chew carefully), burdock (*Arctium lappa*), dandelion roots, yellow dock (*Rumex crispus*), and many other medicinal roots this way.

We collect roots in the autumn, after a frost, in the time of a waning Moon. After washing them in an old washing machine and slicing them in a commercial food processor, we store them in food-grade buckets.

Raspberries are small enough that they dry easily, but strawberries need to be cut in halves or quarters. Tomatoes are best sliced so you can get a nice size once dried that works well in salad or soups. I slice cherry tomatoes in half, which turns out wonderfully. Plum tomatoes (I like Amish Paste tomatoes) work well for drying because they have less moisture in them and are meatier; I quarter these to dry them. Tomatoes are the most popular thing I dry—my friends and family express their appreciation for this gift most enthusiastically.

Store dried berries and tomatoes in the refrigerator or freezer, or you will find moths or larvae in there by midwinter.

The Harvest Moon

Hearing the words *Harvest Moon* kindles a deep sigh for those who live in the North Country. Either a grower feels relieved after the labor of planting, weeding, and bringing in crops, or feels a bit melancholy, with the end drawing near for the joyful harvest and daily garden visits for gathering ingredients for meals, teas, and medicines. The time of turning the corner to shorter days and longer nights has arrived.

The autumnal Harvest Moon has special characteristics that assist the grower and inspire everything. The Harvest Moon is the Full Moon closest to the autumnal equinox. It can occur up to two weeks before or after September 22, and this is either the last Full Moon of summer or the first Full Moon of autumn. The Harvest Moon was especially import-ant in the days before tractors had headlights. Its bright light would extend the hours that could be devoted to outdoor work—especially harvesting. As the season closed, the Full Moon's bright light provided a lamp to the fields and farmers as they labored to bring in the bounty.

There is variation in moonset times as the nights and months pass through the year. Because of the Moon's orbit around the Earth, this variation ranges from about 70 minutes at the solstices to just 25 min-utes at the equinoxes. At the equinox, the orbit of the moon appears to stay closer to our horizon. This gives the farmer another half hour of light each day during the Harvest Moon week. In fact, for those of us that need light most in the northern latitudes as the cold weather blows in, there is a greater Harvest Moon effect: less time between suc-cessive moonrises than in the south, where the season is less dramatic.

How helpful, during those hectic harvest days, to have a Full Moon rise as the Sun sets, keeping the "lights on."

Most seasons of the year have three Full Moons, but often between the summer solstice in June and the autumnal equinox in September, there are four Full Moons. This fourth cycle was the original Blue Moon. Now we refer to the Blue Moon as the second Full Moon in a month. These "extra" Full Moons, the fourth one in three months, usually (but not always) occur in the summer.

Do you recall a time when you saw a gigantic orange Moon rising in the east as the Sun set in the west? The mystique of the Harvest Moon brings memories of larger-than-normal Moons or brighter-colored Moons. The extent of this phenomenon varies from year to year. The path of the Moon—closer to or farther from the horizon—is what determines whether a Full Moon looks bigger or more colorful than usual. The orange color that some Moons carry up to the sky for a short time after moonrise is caused by seeing the Moon through more atmosphere than when we look overhead. As I write this in 2021, we have been experiencing very orange Moons because of western fires; vast areas of land are burning up. The smoke and debris in the atmosphere have made our recent Moons even a brighter shade of orange. The Earth is trying to get our attention, and we need to take more actions, including growing our own food and medicine. These come with no plastic packaging!

Gratitude for the Harvest

These significant and stunning phenomena of planetary movement and beautiful sunsets invoke gratitude for all that Natures bestows on us. It is a shallow point of view to accept the harvest, the extra light at the Full Moon, and dramatically beautiful sunsets without engaging in some kind of reciprocity in gratitude to that which gives us everything we need: Fire, Earth, Air, and Water. The Harvest Moon is the perfect time for giving thanks, for preparing a ceremony to give something back to that which sustains us. It seems appropriate to use some of this time in ceremony, not just in harvesting, yet again taking more from the Earth.

Realizing that from the beginning—seeds—to the bountiful harvest, our gardens are magnificent gifts from Nature puts me in my correct place, full of gratitude, wonder, and curiosity. From this place is where

The Full Moon rising over the Baraboo Bluffs, Wisconsin. Photo by Diane Lasceski-Michaels

you can begin to create your ritual for the Harvest Moon. Instead of heading out to the movies or the mall, or even to the garden to fill up your harvest basket yet again, as the Harvest Moon rises, let's take part in a ritual prepared to show gratitude for that which provides us so much.

Harvest Moon Ritual

It is said that the spirit of Earth does not comprehend human words as well as she does human actions. A major component in gathering materials for a ritual is to engage yourself in the feeling of gratitude. Even in the worst drought year I experienced on our farm, I realized that I could be grateful because I still had more than most. That is a sobering thought but humbling as well. Plus, it puts my heart in a receptive, quiet, and grateful place instead of being upset at my circumstances.

We often look to those who came before us for guidance. So much was lost when European colonizers decimated Indigenous peoples, who had been living in harmony with the Earth, in North America. But I believe that we all can create worthy rituals by engaging our hearts with appropriate gratitude and following our own inspiration in how to show appreciation. In these turbulent times, holding beauty and simplicity seems key. Being here and now, full of love and gratitude, is our proper place as humans. Here are some ideas of elements you could include in your ritual.

Sacred items, such as:

* herbs, such as sage, tobacco (*Nicotiana* spp.), corn meal, artemisias (*Artemisia* spp.), tulsi (*Ocimum tenuiflorum*), rue (*Ruta graveolens*), sweetgrass (*Hierochloe odorata*)
* candles and incense
* flowers
* fruits and vegetables
* prepared foods
* beverages (though, keep a clear head—no alcohol)
* crystals, meaningful stones, or minerals
* bells, singing bowls, music
* paper and pens (for writing down your intentions)

Gather the items you would like to include in your ritual. Find a quiet space that feels comfortable: outdoors in your backyard, in a park, or simply focused on a windowsill decorated for the occasion. Set your intention to express gratitude to Nature, or another intention if you prefer.

Prepare yourself for a ritual. Dress for the occasion. White is a classic color to wear for rituals.

Clear your items with fragrant ceremonial smoke by burning incense, white sage, or sweetgrass over the items. Call in the directions—east, south, west, and north—invoking the energies they offer.

* **East:** Air, inspiration, renewal, enthusiasm
* **South:** Fire, childhood, transformation, action
* **West:** Water, reflection, bounty, unlimited possibilities
* **North:** Earth, balance, wisdom, reflection

Next, you can sing or dance or read some inspirational quotes. Or simply sit in silence to reflect. Now is the time you have set aside to show the Earth and all creation your gratitude. We have much to be grateful for that is so often take for granted. What can you do, moving forward, that would help to support the Earth and give back to that which sustains us?

Reflect on your experience—any internal shifts that took place or inspirations that arose—and write them down.

Try to carry this gratitude forth, as you walk, breathe, and live on this amazing planet filled with beauty and inspiration.

CHAPTER 8

Last Quarter Gardening Activities

It is the marriage of the soul with Nature that makes the intellect fruitful and gives birth to imagination.

—HENRY DAVID THOREAU

You have loved your calendula (*Calendula officinalis*) flowers throughout the entire growing season. They brightened up your garden, made a happy place for butterflies, filled your calendula storage bin for winter salves and creams, and produced some for others. The frost came and all the foliage is brown and crispy. But this row of calendula produced lots of seeds for next year, so here you come with your basket again. One cycle ends and you reflect on its bounty and feel gratitude for the generosity and abundance of Nature as you collect your seeds for the next year's harvest.

It is winter and the Moon just moved into the Last Quarter. I can feel the pull inward. I am getting more inquisitive and introspective. What projects do I need to complete? What garden aspects need my attention most today? How can I clear up communication? Feeling the link between beginnings and endings, it is a day to begin the death-and-destruction phase, so I will work on my gravel paths in the Chakra Planetary Garden. The weeds consume the current gravel paths, and then the garden beds lose their definition. I am going to cover the gravel paths with cardboard to exclude light and air and choke out the weeds as our Wisconsin landscape turns green. Before

135

The Last Quarter Moon by the Numbers

The Last Quarter Moon spans days twenty-two to twenty-five and a half of the lunar cycle. It rises around midnight and sets around noon.

In the Last Quarter, the Moon is getting closer and closer to alignment between the Earth and Sun. Its illuminated portion changes from 90 to 45 degrees.

The Waning Crescent, or Balsamic Moon, begins on day twenty-five of the lunar cycle and lasts until the New Moon, three days during which it fades into darkness. The Moon is aligning between the Earth and the Sun, relinquishing light along the way. From our perspective on Earth, the Moon shrinks to a thin curve, like a C, then disappears completely, changing the illumination from 45 to 0 degrees, complete darkness.

my next tour in a few weeks' time, I will remove the cardboard, and behold! Clear, well-defined paths will be restored, saving my wrists and my time from hours of weeding, while framing the beauty of the plants' colors and textures.

It is an archetypal day of the Last Quarter as I write this. It is a cold April morning, and the low pressure seems to be pushing me back onto the couch, where I can make my nest and rest. These influences are extremely Last Quarter, when many of the planets are in Pisces, the sign of introspection. Neptune, which brings the energy of the deep, emotional ocean, is making me dreamy. Venus is right next to, or conjunct with, Neptune, bringing her soft reflective energy. Mars underscores this entire scene with impulsive energy and Jupiter enhances and expands it.

When you feel lethargic and cannot reach your goals for the day, be kind; you may have several planets working against your goals, or maybe toward your goals but in a mysterious way. Don't worry, go with the flow. Use this time to gather inspiration. This time is not wasted. After all, the word inspire was originally used for a spirit or supernatural being coming to impart a truth or idea. The doors will open for productivity and creation in a week or so. Some consider this the most important Moon phase of all because of its potent visualization potential.

Stargazing during the Last Quarter is an excellent time for introspection and inspiration. It puts me in my place to stargaze, witness the beauty and expansiveness, and wonder at the patterns and flow that have presented themselves to us for eons.

What problems do I have in this wide universe? Are problems not just opportunities for growth? I feel supported in my life by seeing how everything is held in place. Starry skies expand my world to other possibilities not imagined. Often, when we are searching for answers, we feel we are limited to just two possibilities: *this* or *that*. But there is a whole universe of possibilities out there if we take time to stretch and open our minds to feel the support of the One—the energy that holds the Earth, plants, people, and planets all in place, cycling through the universe in perfect rhythm.

This Last Quarter resting time corresponds with inward winter and seeds. This is a quiet time for reassessing your plans—but also for killing things like weeds and pests. This destruction need not be dismal; after all, endings come before beginnings, and we all need compost!

The Balsamic Moon

The Balsamic Moon, also called the Waning Crescent, is like incense dissolving into the ethers. It pulls you into dreamtime. Half-asleep, half-awake is normal for this part of the monthly cycle. This is the time to enjoy your hammock or resting place, to observe and appreciate your garden. Who knows, this time is so dreamy, you may see an unknown flash of light or perhaps a garden fairy hiding nearby. This is when the veils between the worlds are thin.

Think of balsamic vinegar. Traditional balsamic vinegar is made by aging it for twelve to twenty-five years underground. That offers a vision of what this phase does best—go and hibernate.

Drink some water. Our bodies hold less moisture during the Balsamic phase, so rehydrating is important.

A Balsamic Moon energizes the deepest part of your dreamtime, influencing intuition and instinct. Use this time to dream, not act.

Dana Gerhardt, a contemporary astrological writer, believes that if you practice and honor one Moon phase, this should be the one.

> Remember having a particularly exhausting day, and that night, how good it felt to turn off the lights and drop your weary body into bed, sloughing off the chattering thoughts? Remember how good it felt next morning, waking up refreshed and renewed, your problems shrunk to their rightful size, your optimism and hope grown larger?*

This describes the value of taking time out for inaction and intuition, revering time for renewal.

Planning one's life and activities can flow much smoother when following the energy of the Moon phases. This rhythm also helps organize activities throughout the month to keep life in balance and cover all the bases, not just gravitating toward your favorite pursuits. The monthly cycle of the Moon has made my gardens, home, and life more organized and efficient, noticing and acting when it is time for expansion and time for contraction.

This time of transition is the best time for creative problem-solving. In this dark Moon phase, solo, quiet time is essential. This is "the space between worlds," as noted contemporary astrologer and author Steven Forrest describes in his book *The Book of the Moon*. Seek out your guided messages, but as Forrest warns, "Be careful to not let this lead you into self-absorption or self-pity." I find that resting (or vacationing) is usually a good cure for this ailment because, after a good rest, I feel renewed and ready to get on with my inspirations.

A Non-Planting Phase

The Last Quarter is a nonplanting time. Instead, turn your attention to cultivation, weeding, and setting traps. This is a good time to harvest for drying fruits, vegetables, and medicine because the Last Quarter

---

* Dana Gerhardt, "Moon Watching Series (9): The Balsamic Moon," Astrodienst, accessed June 22, 2023, https://www.astro.com/astrology/in_dg_balsamic_e.htm.

has everything locked up and stored in plant tissues. The plants have less moisture in the cells and are easier to dry. Potassium absorbs better into the soil applied during the Last Quarter.

Because the Last Quarter is considered a resting period, it is a good time to prune to reduce growth. I used to have a Blackhaw Viburnum (*Viburnum prunifolium*) hedge at the back of my house. In time, it grew so large that it started blocking the view through the windows on my porch. I needed to trim back the hedge, but with limited time, I could only dedicate one day a year to that project. On a Last Quarter day during a Leo Moon, I brandished my pruning shears and cut back the viburnum to a level right below the windows. This worked like magic, stunting the viburnum for months, until next spring's flush of growth. I have used this phase for the purpose of pruning to reduce growth ever since.

During the Last Quarter, Earth's energy draws in. The water table continues falling during this phase, creating lighter and more receptive soil. (Keep in mind that water weighs about 8 pounds per gallon [3.6 kg/3.8 L].) Early Chinese farmers used this time of soil weight lightening to their advantage when tilling with primitive plows. The water buffalo they used as draft animals would not get as tired out when plowing during the Last Quarter. Anyone who has worked in wet soil knows how incredibly heavy it is! Take advantage of this lowered water table for time-saving and efficiency in eliminating weeds. Those pesky weeds will have less water available to reestablish their roots.

The openness of the soil in the Last Quarter is also favorable for adding organic matter or fertilizing with organic products. Fertilizers break down faster at this time and are absorbed into the soil more efficiently, similar to the previous week,

Keywords for the Last Quarter

Finding solitude
Serving
Finding the poignant
Finding impermanence
Transcending
Detaching
Meditating
Feeling the psychic
Creating
Imagining the visionary

More Gardening Tips for the Last Quarter

★ Cultivate to kill weeds. Leo and Gemini, the drier Air and Fire signs, are better for destroying weeds, setting traps, or other activities that eliminate growth. The best sign for pulling weeds is Capricorn, between January and July, in the Last Quarter.

★ Fertilize soil for root growth on Earth sign days (Taurus, Virgo, and Capricorn) or for leaf growth on Water sign days (Cancer, Scorpio, and Pisces). Occasionally fertilize for flowers on flower days (Air signs: Gemini, Libra, and Aquarius). Fertilize for grains on Fire days (Aries and Sagittarius), but avoid Leo, because the fixed Fire is too hot-natured.

★ Cut back trees and hedges to decrease growth, especially when the Moon is descending (Gemini to Sagittarius).

★ Destroy unwanted growth in a barren sign (Fire and Air signs, plus Virgo). Mow lawns now, and you'll be rewarded with slower regrowth.

★ Prune fruit trees on a fruit day, in the Fire signs of Aries, Leo, and Sagittarius.

★ Divide perennials while they are resting; they will heal more quickly.

★ Collect medicinal bark in the spring or autumn.

★ Harvest produce going directly into storage, as with potatoes, onions, and apples. The signs of Aries, Sagittarius, or Aquarius are preferred because these are the weaker of the barren signs. Note this is not for your current needs but for storage purposes.

★ Order seeds and organize your seed collection.

★ Complete old structures or projects.

★ Collect roots during a Balsamic Moon, especially in late autumn or early spring.

★ Clean out a junk drawer, garage or garden shed, especially in a Virgo Moon. Throw out old catalogs, old packets of seeds, and broken tools.

★ Cut wood for burning in your woodstove or outdoor fire pit; it will be drier during this phase.
★ Sit with plants and draw them in a sketchbook; this helps bring you into closer relationship with the plants.
★ Preserve fruits by canning; they will be less juicy but will hold up well in storage because of the lower moisture content.
★ Prepare mineral-rich herbal infusions to nourish the blood.
★ Transmute negativity into good for all. Let go.
★ Ponder a plan to release old habits; go inward; dream.

just past the Full Moon. It's a general rule of thumb to add fertilizer to the soil ten days before planting so the microbiome can start to incorporate it into the soil. This timing is perfect since the upcoming New Moon and First Quarter will favor planting. The Last Quarter is a good time to plow down cover crops, side-dress with organic fertilizers such as compost, pelletized manure products (I use Suståne, pelletized turkey manure), bat guano, worm castings, fish emulsion, or whatever organic fertilizer you prefer or can find locally.

Also during this quieter time, pay attention to what you really need to plant and harvest from your garden. For years I planted one hundred cabbage plants because I thought they were so beautiful together, they looked like a bouquet of roses to my adoring eyes. Wherever I went I gave people gifts of fresh cabbage heads. Eventually, though, large populations of flea beetles built up and began to destroy my cabbage transplants. Even though I moved my small cabbage, broccoli, and cauliflower transplants to a different area of my farm, the flea beetles found them and feasted on them. Because of this pest imbalance that I inadvertently created, I must now wait and plant only a late crop of cabbage-family plants, after the flea beetle population has decreased.

Because the Last Quarter is also a good time to fight pests, you may want to plan ahead and make a pest-fighting herbal infusion to use during this period. Gather some potent insecticidal or repellent plants such as the ones listed in Table 8.1. For the simplest method to brew an

Table 8.1 Organic Infusions to Deter Pests

Pest	Ingredients for Pest-Fighting Infusion
aphids	stinging nettle (*Urtica* spp.)
cabbage moths	mugwort (*Artemisia vulgaris*), peppermint (*Mentha piperita*), sage (*Salvia officinalis*), tomato leaves, thyme (*Thymus vulgaris*)
flea beetles	elderflower (*Sambucus nigra*), garlic, onions, peppermint, wormwood (*Artemisia absinthium*)
mice	garlic, peppermint
mildew	basil, chives, garlic

herbal infusion, pour boiling water over the plants and let it sit overnight to steep. Then spray a diluted solution (1:4 to 1:10 solution to water) of the infusion on the areas in your garden where pests are a problem.

My preferred method, though, is to set a 5-gallon (19 L) bucket half full of water in my garden near the plants that are infested with pests. I add the aromatic, repellent plant material to the water and let it sit for several days, stirring daily. Soon it will break down and start fermenting. You can then spray this liquid on the plants, or if you are lucky, you may have the same experience I have had. One spring, I put some old, sprouting garlic cloves, some leftover hot peppers that had never gotten processed, and some wormwood (*Artemisia absinthium*) foliage in the bucket of water. The pests on my crop left the area without me even having to spray, that bucket stunk so much!

A Time to Design

This dreamy Last Quarter is a good time to conjure up a garden design. What type of garden do you want to create to support your body, spirit, or landscape? I consider any type of garden a sanctuary, whether it be a formal display garden or a planter full of herbs and flowers on a balcony. As you generate ideas, think about the connections between the qualities offered by the plant world and how those qualities support humans.

Designing a garden begins with considering your needs and available space but also provides a link to feed your soul. Just thinking and planning

Design Arises from Observation

Before you start to create a garden plan, take time to observe.

Observe some gardens around you. Notice that a garden is alive and can be unruly, like a puppy or playful child. It changes from year to year, but it always is a source of company, joy, beauty, and exercise.

Then turn your gaze inward.

Observe a need. Do you need medicine, food for the body, or food for the soul (meaning flowers)? How can your garden meet those needs? What do you want to create in the space you have?

a garden can be levitating to the spirit! Let's take a garden design journey.

Imagine your life with a space for expansion of your higher self. A space created with plants you feel an affinity with, plants that speak to your psyche or pique an area of interest. Feel the tranquility and clarity that arises from your sacred space, connecting you to Nature and all that is. Creating this design can tap into your inner wisdom and needs.

Nature connects us to well-being. After all, many powerful remedies are easy to grow from seeds or are already growing wild around us. Some are even considered weeds, trampled underfoot. Colors, textures, and sounds of Nature offer harmony and balance. Pause; be attentive to the natural world; engage and pay attention! This may give you clues as to what you need to find peace and joy. You can create a space, large or small, by intentionally adding some plants that lift your spirits. Which plants speak to you: scented, medicinal, colorful, statuesque, edible, beautiful, or plants that offer sheer delight?

Gardening with a theme makes the project of designing a garden more fun and educational. Research your area of interest and expand your plant possibilities. Here are some ideas for a themed garden.

* tea garden
* fragrant garden
* culinary garden

* medicinal garden
* biblical or meditation garden
* butterfly garden
* Four Directions or humors garden
* chakra planetary garden

I created sample plant lists for most of these theme gardens (see Appendix 1: Themed Garden Plant Lists). And chapter 9 is devoted to the story of how I designed and installed a chakra planetary garden near my home, including a detailed plan of the garden.

Create a Sanctuary Garden

A sanctuary is a safe haven created for contemplation. Nature is the venue for experiencing the marvels of the universe, from an unfolding flower to a sunset. We need time to be still, quiet, and receptive for mental clarity. Nature opens us up to a world of possibilities and unlimited solutions.

Our twenty-first-century society is dominated by the push toward materialism, commercialism, and technology. This is another reason to create a sanctuary. "The earth needs us to wake up. Our relationship to the land is broken," writes Robin Wall Kimmerer in *Braiding Sweetgrass*. The simple act of selecting a few plants that spark your interest can help you to connect back to that which truly sustains all life. We need to create sanctuary spaces for ourselves and for the planet. As gardeners, we have a relationship with the Earth. Think about planting seeds to create beauty that will lift your spirit and will touch others who are known to you, but also for the spirits of many who are *unknown*. And any size garden supports pollinators in the web of life, for example, a pot of zinnias or cosmos flowers.

Site Selection

Whether your goal is to redesign your whole yard or simply to create a grouping of potted plants, you can select something that will inspire you and elevate your days, be it fragrance, color, beauty, food, or medicine.

To begin, consider the shape, age, and appearance of your dwelling. This will help you determine what style of garden would enhance the

Perennials like these stunning lupines are great for early bloom, but their show lasts for only a few weeks. Fill in your perennial border with annuals like dianthus and nasturtiums for added interest throughout the season. Photo by Diane Lasceski-Michaels

surroundings. A country home makes me think of a kitchen garden design, while a smaller suburban landscape might be enhanced by something more formal. But don't forget: formality and informality can enhance and complement one another.

What size area do you want to develop? This will help determine the shape of the garden, which in turn will begin to formulate the bones of the design. Consider your soil and climate. Whether your soil is sandy or clay-rich, adding organic matter offers benefits: it improves the ability of sandy soil to hold water and nutrients, and it improves porosity and aeration in clay soil. Understanding the patterns of your local weather and climate will help you make better plant choices.

Observe the landscape at different seasons and different times of day: after a light snow, in the late evening and early morning when shadows make nuances pop. This variation shines a light on how the components of your garden will be perceived and how to accentuate focal points.

Observe your garden site to see which parts of it are shaded and which are in full sun. Take note of the changes in sun and shade patterns over the course of the day, and over the whole growing season, if possible. This will help you fine-tune your plant selection—you may discover that you should choose more shade-tolerant plants than you expected, for example.

What plants or themes inspire you? This is where the fun begins! Research your area of interest and pick your favorite species within that theme. Make a list and see how they fit together in your design, blending heights, cultural requirements, perennials, and annuals. Always blend annuals in with perennials if possible. Annuals add the desired color throughout the growing season, while perennials flower for a shorter period but add interesting textures with a great selection of flowers to choose from.

Elements of Formality

The infrastructure present in the site or what you add determines a formal design. Installing walls, trellises, or hedges provides privacy and protection for your sacred space. Adding fountains, exotic plants, topiaries, and various heights of trimmed hedges accentuate formality.

Statues representing the theme provide focal points to draw the eyes to a particular set point in the garden, giving the eyes a spot to rest and soak in the beauty, and the mind a place to wander.

Areas of mowed lawn accentuate a garden. A lovely stretch of lawn invites visitors to stroll, to sit down and contemplate the garden, or to lay back and daydream.

Elements of Informality

Informal does not mean haphazard. Informality is gentle and blends lines, textures, and dimensions, like Nature does, creating ease, relaxation, and joy for the viewer. "Not chaos-like together crushed and bruised, but, as the world, harmoniously confused: where order in variety we see, and where, though all things differ, all agree." These words from eighteenth-century English poet Alexander Pope perfectly describe an informal garden. An informal design includes slopes, curved lines, and various heights of plants, all complementing one another. Trees and shrubs are placed irregularly and accentuated with perennials and annuals. Utilitarian structures, like a garden shed, fit in well with the feeling of an informal design. Mix it up—while maintaining a flowing plan—and adapt the style and design within the environment.

Sounds. Sounds affect your mind and emotions. Compare a siren to a babbling brook and it is easy to discern what is appealing. Bring calming sounds to your sanctuary garden to enhance the meditative experience. Singing birds are a sign all is safe, which soothes the soul to release worry and stress. The screech of a red-tailed hawk, my totem animal, seems to greet me often on my country road, sometimes even flying above my car for a bit, matching my speed.

Soothing sounds encourage alpha brain waves, which open the mind to a relaxed focus and an unconscious wisdom. People are more productive in this calm, clear-thinking mode. Add implements for meditative sounds, such as chimes, water features, or a gong, or features that will attract birds (and hence, birdsong), such as bird feeders, baths, and houses.

Scents. Scent is linked to the oldest part of the brain, the limbic system, or the reptilian brain. This governs behavior and long-term

As you sketch out a design, you can dream ahead to the day you'll plant your garden and bring your creative vision to life. Photo by Diane Lasceski-Michaels

memory. To this day, I distinctly remember the smells of my grand-mother's house: bread baking in the oven, the oil in her humming sewing machine, and Viceroy cigarettes.

Scent is another thing Nature does best. Nature's scents are sub-tle, distinctive, seductive, and elusively in the moment. According to the Sleep Foundation, odors can affect our dreams, with studies showing that pleasant dreams arise when floral scents are nearby.

Do you know it is impossible to extract the scent of lilacs? Per-fumers have tried for centuries. *Do* take time to smell the flowers when they are in bloom. Who knows, tomorrow may be cloudy or cooler and the peak degree of scent will be gone, not to come again for another year.

Colors. Colors evoke various internal responses, and preferences can change with the seasons. "What color do I feel like wearing today?" exemplifies this feeling of color and mood. It's great to have choices in life and with plants, such as choosing annuals to offer a blast of summery colors. Perennials, shrubs, and trees can provide structure and some color, but annuals accentuate and bring a pop of color all summer long. Here is a list of colors and the emotions they evoke.

* ★ **red:** love, pleasure, power, passion, prosperity
* ★ **orange:** happiness, warmth, sociability, enthusiasm, courage, sensuality, vitality
* ★ **yellow:** happiness, personal power, will, optimism, cheer
* ★ **white:** purity, virtue, calm, clarity, new beginnings
* ★ **green:** contentment, relief, growth, abundance, heart-centered, compassion, balance, peace
* ★ **violet:** knowingness, wisdom, inspiration, meditation
* ★ **sky blue:** communication, creative expression, friendliness, peace, security
* ★ **indigo:** intuition, perception, fearlessness, vision

Design Time

Once you have decided on a theme that excites you (which can be as simple as a single word, like *peace*), it's time to begin planning your design on paper.

Gather the materials you'll need:

* ★ pencil and eraser
* ★ large sheet of paper (gridlines are helpful)
* ★ ruler or straight edge
* ★ drawing board (that you can carry)
* ★ long tape measure
* ★ a stake (to hold down one end of the tape measure)

Decide on an overall dimension of your garden site, either by measuring with your tape measure or by step-measuring. (An average person's step length is 1½ to 2 feet [46–61 cm].) If your garden is small

Fragrant Plants

Consider planting some of these wonderfully fragrant plants in a bed or container near a window of your home.

Annuals/Perennials
jasmine (*Jasminum grandiflorum*)
rose geranium (*Pelargonium graveolens*)
lemon verbena (*Aloysia citrodora*)
common stock (*Matthiola incana*)
sweet peas (*Lathyrus odoratus*)
lavender (*Lavandula angustifolia*)
artemisias (*Artemisia* spp.)*

Shrubs/Vines
roses (*Rosa* spp.)
lilacs (*Syringa* spp.)
alpine currant (*Ribes alpinum*)
Korean spice viburnum (*Viburnum carlesii*)
mock orange (*Philadelphus coronarius*)

---

* Avoid mugwort (*Artemisia vulgaris*) planted in a garden because it spreads aggressively.

enough to guestimate the size, you can skip measuring it out. Next, draw the design. Put fixed items in first, like your home, a bench, your garden shed, and paved paths. Note where the windows are and what views you want to feature. Then fill in the established trees and shrubs. Consider the boundaries of your space. Note topography and microclimates. For example, is there a low spot that would hold moisture for water-loving plants, or shady areas for shade-tolerant or woodland plants?

Think about screens that can hold the space in which the garden will reside. Possibilities for screening include walls, fences, gates, vines (such as hops [*Humulus lupulus*], wisteria [*Wisteria* spp.], grape), columnar trees, or a hedge. The screen itself should blend in with the surroundings.

The Doctrine of Signatures

The Last Quarter and Balsamic Moon are introspective times that can enhance your experience in learning about what is called the Doctrine of Signatures.

The Doctrine of Signatures is an ancient system of observation, of looking closely and with intuition to uncover the uses of plants. Does the yellow in a dandelion imply it may assist in liver function? Does the shape of a ginkgo leaf imply it may bring blood to the brain and aid its function? This is called a heuristic tool—for thinking, observing, and discovering for yourself. Many herbalists find this approach to observation as valid as taking precise measurements of plant constituents in a lab. For more information, I recommend Julia Graves's *The Language of Plants*.

In postmodern Western culture, we are trained to not trust our own intuition. We are constantly told that we are less than complete until we buy the next thing. But plants, planets, and the world of Nature gently invite us to look closely. By returning to Nature, we can find seductive beauty and rhythm, which can restore the balance where "elite" humans are not the ones who matter most but all living things are equal and deserve consideration. A recent conversation with herbalists Matt Wood, Margi Flint, and Jim McDonald revealed that each one of us experiences seemingly magical situations that arise when looking closely at Nature. So many answers and needs are supplied effortlessly by showing up and paying attention to Nature. I think that other cultures teach this knowledge, but it would never work in a capitalistic society because we would not feel a need to buy many things.

In every era, the Doctrine of Signatures has had its skeptics. While plants do have a cornucopia of medicinal properties, historically assigned signatures are fascinating, at the very least, and these observations make useful and memorable connections for uncovering plant uses.

Don't be intimidated to have a dialog with the plants. Two of my best-selling products came from recipes that the plants whispered to me in the Balsamic Moon. As insightful herbalist and astrologer Will Morris says in his book *Cycles in Medical Astrology*, "The use of science to dismiss the Doctrine of Signatures is no different from science as a tool of the empire."

In *Monocultures of the Mind*, Indian agricultural activist and physicist Vandana Shiva writes:

> Dominant scientific knowledge thus breeds a monoculture of the mind by making space for local alternatives to disappear, very much like monocultures of introduced plant varieties leading to the displacement and destruction of local diversity. . . . By elevating itself above society and other knowledge systems . . . from the domain of reliable and systematic knowledge the dominant systems create its exclusive monopoly.

Let's find our way back to the Sacred Mystery of all life. Discover through introspection how to create the best possible outcome for all involved. Release and prepare for new beginnings.

CHAPTER 9

Mark the Seasons with Tonics and Treats

I adore living with four distinct seasons and feeling the energy moving through them. The seasons provide a rhythm of beginnings, growth, fruition, and rest. Each season is marked by special activities. For me as a northerner, winter is a bit too long, but we look forward to making maple syrup in March and April. It gets us outdoors after the frigid months, and boiling sap in the woods over a fire brings contentment, plus all that syrup!

Maple sugaring segues into starting seeds, filling the greenhouse with herb, vegetable, and flower transplants in the spring. In early summer comes plant sales and planting the fields. We tend the plants for the next month or two and reap the rewards with our bushels of harvest.

In late summer we are canning, freezing, pickling, and fermenting to prepare for winter. Our basement pantry is overflowing! In autumn, we haul in the root crops and squashes. Then, it is finally time for holidays and rest. It is a joy to host gatherings where we serve all the abundant health and flavors from our gardens.

Winter is a time for writing, studying, and going inward to refocus and orient my goals. This quiet season provides clear insights that are harder to access during the busier times of year. I am getting much better at taking time for reflection and tuning in to the monthly New Moon cycle.

A great way to honor each season, monthly Full Moon and New Moon energies, and the solstices and equinoxes, is to go into Nature, receive her gifts of bounty, and create something that captures the moment. In this chapter, I share some of my best recipes for seasonal herbal syrups and other tonics. These thoughtful creations are always shared with others—I love to spread the joy and the health-giving properties of these recipes. When you make them, be sure you make enough to give some away! Reciprocity truly is a way of jumping into the circle of life. People sometimes tell me I am generous, and I always respond, "I have the best teacher and example—Nature."

Recipes for Spring

Dandelion and Yellow Dock Mighty Mix

Collect yellow dock and dandelion roots and leaves in the spring or fall and use some immediately to make this syrup, which you can take by the tablespoon daily or twice a week to help fortify the blood.

Yellow dock (*Rumex crispus*) roots	Water
Dandelion leaves and roots	Molasses

Wash the yellow dock and dandelion roots and leaves thoroughly. Chop the roots into ½- to 1-inch (13–25 mm) chunks.

Place the roots and leaves in a large pot. For every 1 cup (240 mL) chopped roots, add 1 quart (960 mL) water. Bring to a boil, then turn down the heat and simmer until the volume is reduced by about half. Then remove from the heat and let the decoction sit overnight.

The next morning, simmer down halfway again. Strain the liquid, discarding the roots and leaves. Measure the quantity of strained liquid, and then add an equal amount of molasses to it.

Return the decoction to the stove and warm it gently over low heat, stirring to dissolve the molasses.

Pour the finished decoction into a glass jar with a tight-fitting lid. Label the jar with the mix's name, ingredients, date, and the day's astrological influence. It will keep for about one year in the refrigerator.

Make or take this decoction under a Jupiter influence (Sagittarius, Pisces), which rules the liver. Make or take under a Mars influence (Aries, Scorpio) for vitality and vigor.

Violet Syrup

When I want to make this syrup, I simply take a jar out to my violet patch and pick until the jar is full.

Freshly picked violet
   (*Viola* spp.) flowers
Water

Honey
Lemon juice (optional)

Fill a pint or quart jar with violet flowers. Boil water and pour it over the violets, filling the jar to 1 inch (2.5 cm) below the rim. Let the jar sit and infuse for 1 hour to overnight. Strain out the flowers.

Add honey: ½ cup (120 mL) for a pint jar; 1 cup (240 mL) for a quart jar. Warm gently to dissolve the honey into the infusion.

If you want to tint the syrup to a more fuchsia color, add a squeeze of lemon juice. I never do this, though, because I adore the clear violet hue of the untinted syrup. Maybe for a pre-teen birthday party, when the color featured has more pink tones, this may suit the situation.

A spoonful of this enchanting syrup in sparkling water or a martini creates a sweet memory for guests. Photo courtesy of Lillian Sizemore

155

Pour the infusion in your prettiest jar or bottle, and label with ingredients, date, and Moon sign. Keep refrigerated; it will keep for up to one year.

Venus or Neptune rules violets, so to potentize this to the planets, you can make or take this blend under a Neptunian influence (Pisces). Make or take it under a Venus influence (Taurus, Libra) to further invoke the feeling you get while gazing at this elegant elixir.

Recipes for Summer

Summer is time for outdoor picnics and elegant cocktails or mocktails, straight from the garden. Guests appreciate being served delicacies you create using fresh flowers and herbs harvested from your garden.

Elderflower fizz is a refreshing drink for a late summer afternoon. Photo courtesy of Lillian Sizemore

Elderflower Fizz

The dog days of summer are known as the hottest days of the season, landing in late July and early August. I always thought that the dog days were so named because the weather was so hot, even dogs would spend their time lazing about and taking naps in the shade. Wrong! Sirius, the Dog Star, belongs to the constellation Canis Major (aka the Greater Dog) and is the brightest star in the sky. The "dog days" are named for Sirius, which rises and sets with the Sun at this time of year. This potent Star was believed to contribute to the days' heat (although scientifically speaking, it does not). Some sources name the dog days as the period from about July 3 through August 11, spanning 20 days before and 20 days after the date on which Sirius rises and falls in conjunction with the Sun.

These hot days fall right when your Elderflower Fizz is ready. Get some ice and seltzer to cool down your Fizz and relax in your garden's shade, soaking in the beauty.

1 gallon (3.8 L) water
1½ pounds (680 g) sugar
1 organic lemon

12 large elderflower (*Sambucus canadensis* or *S. nigra*) heads (botanically, cymes, a flower cluster with a central stem)

Heat the water in a large pot and add the sugar, stirring until the sugar dissolves. Allow to cool to room temperature. Squeeze in all the juice from the lemon and add the rind to the liquid as well.

Place the elderflower blossoms in a sterilized glass jar or bottle, then add the sweetened water with lemon rind to the elderflowers. (I recommend glass instead of plastic because of the chemicals that leach out of plastic.) It's important to open the bottle each day or every couple of days to release the gases, if they have a tight seal.

Leave covered for 10 to 14 days, then strain. The carbonic acid creates an effervescent and refreshing beverage. This beverage can be stored for up to a year, but you should make sure the fermentation is finished before you really tighten the lids. If your container is large and you want to store a portion of the beverage after enjoying some, pour it into a smaller container so you don't lose the bubbles, like you can with club soda.

Make or serve under a Venus Moon (Taurus, Libra, Pisces) to enhance your elegant experience.

Mugolio or Pine-Cone Syrup

The timing for making this syrup varies greatly according to what Zone you are in, what species of conifers grow in your region, and the weather conditions. (Drought tends to speed up the flowering and fruiting of plants.)

Collect green (or purple) pine or spruce cones as they are developing. This recipe will not work if you use brown cones found in the late summer to winter.

Green pine or spruce cones	Brown sugar, turbinado sugar, or maple sugar

Collect enough cones to fill a quart jar. Rinse them and drain (no need to dry them for the next step), and return to the jar. Pour in enough sugar to cover the cones. Shake the jar. Alternatively, layer the cones with the sugar as you fill the jar with an alternating layer of each.

Cover the jar and put it in a sunny spot, preferably outdoors, and leave it there for 30 days.

Water will exude out of the cones, dissolving the sugar and extracting the delicious resinous constituents. This will begin to ferment, so you will need to open the jar every few days to release the pressure.

After 30 days, you may need to transfer the whole batch to a stainless-steel pot and heat it gently to ensure all the sugar is dissolved.

Strain the liquid and pour it into dark apothecary bottles. (The tinted glass does not let in light and helps hold the color.) Label with name, ingredients, date, and the day's astrological influence. Keep refrigerated for up to 1 year.

Make or take under a Gemini influence, which rules the bronchiole tubes and upper lung, or under a Jupiter influence (Sagittarius, Pisces, and Cancer) to move congestion out.

Fruit and Herb Cordials

This is a sweetened way to preserve fruits for beverages. Elderberry, raspberry, Cornelian cherry (Cornus mas), wild cherry (Prunus serotina), hawthorn (Crataegus spp.), blueberry, or any other edible fruit works well for making these cordials. Collect your fruits with love and appreciation. What a gift these plants are! Fruit is created with all this beauty and abundance, as well as blood-building nutrients, in gorgeous compostable packages. I like to add it to seltzer or club soda, or use it in cocktails to intensify the colors and add medicinal qualities.

Mixed fresh berries and fruit
  of your choice
Water

Sugar or honey
Brandy

Wash the fruit and place it in an enamel or stainless-steel pot. For every 1 quart (960 mL) of fruit, add 1½ quarts (1.4 L) water and 2 to 4 cups (480–960 mL) of sugar or honey. Simmer gently for 45 minutes, stirring frequently.

Put the fruits and liquid in a strainer to remove the seeds and skins. You can use a food mill, such as for applesauce or tomatoes or push the cooked fruit through a loose fabric, like muslin.

Add the pressed fruit pulp back into the pot (compost the seeds and skins). Cook over low to medium heat until the mixture thickens to the right consistency. (You choose the right consistency.) I like it a bit thickened, like a refrigerated syrup.

Measure the evaporated fruit mixture to determine the total quantity you have made. Add brandy in an amount equal to 50 percent of the total volume of the sweetened fruit mixture. That is, for every 1 cup (240 mL) of mixture, add ½ cup (120 mL) brandy.

Decant the cordial into your favorite glass bottles. Label with name, ingredients, date, and the day's astrological influence. Keep refrigerated. The cordial will keep for up to a year in the refrigerator.

Make or take under a Jupiter influence (Sagittarius, Pisces, Cancer) for longevity, levity, and vitality. Make or take under a Mars influence (Aries, Scorpio, Capricorn) for strength, immune support, and stamina.

Recipes for Autumn

The days are growing shorter, the temperatures are shifting. Time to gather the abundance that's outdoors to bring in for increased winter health.

Elderberry Syrup

Elderberries must be destemmed before using them in a recipe. Some people say the fruits come off the stems easier if they are frozen first. In my opinion, it does not make a difference.

4 cups (960 mL) organic
   elderberries, destemmed
4 cups (960 mL) water
1- to 2- inch (2.5–5 cm) piece
   fresh ginger root, grated
   or chopped

1 cinnamon stick
Honey
Brandy

Place the elderberries and water in a stainless-steel pot with the ginger root and cinnamon stick. Simmer for 30 minutes, covered.

Cover and let the mixture steep overnight. Strain off the fruit, ginger root, and cinnamon stick. Measure the amount of liquid you have and return the pot. Gently warm it as you add 2 cups (480 mL) of honey for every 1 quart (960 mL) of juice. Cool to room temperature. Add 2 cups of brandy for every 1 quart of juice. Stir well.

Pour the liquid into bottles. Label with name, ingredients, date, and the day's astrological influence. Keep refrigerated for up to 1 year. And the next year, you can make another fresh batch.

Make or take under a Mercury influence (Gemini, Virgo, Aquarius), which rules healing and medicine, for general health, or under a Jupiter influence (Sagittarius, Pisces, Cancer), which is associated with fruits, for more potency.

Cherry-Bark Cough Syrup

Collect wild black cherry (Prunus serotina)*, pin cherry* (Prunus pensylvanica)*, or chokecherry* (Prunus virginiana) *bark in the autumn, when the leaves are falling off the trees. Autumn is when the potency of the wild cherry tree travels down the bark, headed to the roots to be stored over winter. What a generous gift of Nature: a natural substance contained in cherry bark that assists with the hacking coughs of winter, and it is at arm's reach, for free! Now it is up to you to fill your heart with gratitude at the generosity and wisdom that grows on trees as you approach them.*

Dried cherry bark is the source of an effective and soothing natural cough syrup.

Collect small branches, 1 inch (2.5 cm) in diameter or less, using loppers or a hand saw.

Six branches at 3 to 5 feet (.9–1.5 m) long will offer you plenty of bark. Using a potato peeler, peel off the bark, taking care to get the green inner bark, and not just the inert, outer, dark, paper-thin bark (often covered with raised, white speckles called lenticels*). The bark will smell like almond extract being poured from a bottle—both almond and cherry are in the* Prunus *genus.*

Once you have collected a quart jar's worth of bark, you have enough material to make 1½ to 2 quarts (1.4–1.9 L) of cough syrup.

Most barks, seeds, and roots need to be simmered for a long time to release their constituents, but cherry bark contains volatile oils that can be lost by simmering too long.

1 quart (960 mL) cherry bark 2 cups (480 mL) honey
1½ quarts (1.4 L) water 2 cups (480 mL) brandy

Measure out a fully packed 1-quart jar of bark, rinse the bark, and empty the bark into a stainless-steel or enamel pot. Cover with the water. Simmer for 15 minutes, covered.

161

Let the decoction sit overnight, covered, so it can release all constituents into the liquid.

Strain the liquid and then return it to the stove to warm as you add the honey. Stir until all the honey dissolves.

Allow the sweetened liquid to cool to room temperature. Stir in the brandy.

Pour into dark apothecary jars. Label with name, ingredients, date, and the day's astrological influence. Keep refrigerated. Mine has stored well for beyond a year.

Make or take under a Mercury influence (Gemini, Virgo, Aquarius), which rules healing and medicine, for more potency.

Potent Plant Powder

The days grow shorter as the autumn equinox approaches. Although you cooked all summer with your fresh culinary herbs, there is an abundance left in your garden. Sometimes it feels like too much to collect each one, dry them separately, grind them, find jars, and write labels just so you can store them away in a cupboard.

This is my kind of recipe! Making this seasoning powder is an efficient way to simplify the harvest of your culinary herbs. Take a paper grocery bag and pruners out to your garden. Stroll around your culinary herbs, appreciating their flavors, beauty, and medicinal qualities. Begin to fill your bag with a culinary blend in mind. Harvest all the leaves that are clean. You want to avoid leaves that are holding any soil, so skip the bottom third of the plant, which can go back to the Earth at the end of the season. Those stems and leaves will trap snow to provide cover for overwintering and protect the crowns of perennial herbs from drying winds.

Options for an Italian blend (which could also be called Herbes de Jardin, *or Herb Blend from Gaia) are:*

Basils (*Ocimum* spp.)	Sage (*Salvia officinalis*)
Hyssop (*Hyssopus officinalis*)	Savory, winter (*Satureja montana*)
Parsley (*Petroselinum crispum*)	or summer (*S. hortensis*)
Rosemary (*Rosmarinus*	Thyme (*Thymus vulgaris*) or
officinalis)	lemon thyme (*T. citriodorus*)

You may be surprised to see hyssop on this list. I hesitated to try it myself because it tastes so bitter—I thought of it as a cough remedy. But I discovered that the bitter quality made the other flavors pop, and this has become my favorite autumn culinary blend.

Put the bag in a dry, warm place, such as an upstairs bedroom or on the top of a refrigerator. When the herbs are dried, you can just crunch the sides of the bag together to garble or destem the herbs. This way, you don't have to fuss with every stem, the leaves fall off with this crushing action. I have started pulverizing the leaves in a food processor after removing them from the bag for easier bottling and use.

This list is a guide, not definitive. Use your intuition and creativity to create your own blend. It's fun!

I use this powder in soups and on popcorn, frozen pizza, and Italian dishes. When I use this blend, I say that my soups are a delicious version of a flu shot. Culinary herbs are potent, too!

Wreaths for All Seasons

I have made herbal wreaths based on the language of flowers by Margaret Pickson for decades. I love the old folklore of plants, which links back to earlier knowledge that has been lost in our modern Western culture. Folklore

Making traditional evergreen wreaths is a wintertime project, but an herbal wreath can be made any time of year.

of plants opens doors to imagination, possibilities, and giving love with herbs in another way. Assembling the scents, textures, colors, and meanings is a great way to share your garden and uplift the spirits of friends.

I recommend that you use a wreath frame (I like the wire ones) and florist wire for making your wreath. A string could work in place of florist wire, but be sure to pull the string very tight, especially when working with fresh material, which shrinks as it dries and can come loose if not tightly affixed.

What sentiment do you want to offer the recipient of your bounty? Make a list of what plants you have available and what sentiment you want to offer. You can find lists of herbs for births and other occasions in Appendix 2. Artemisias are my favorite base material for a wreath because they are extremely fragrant, abundant, and flexible when fresh. Sage and conifers are also good.

Here's an example of a plant list for a wedding wreath:

Agrimony for thankfulness

Amaranth for unfading love

Arborvitae for
  unchanging friendship

Chrysanthemum for cheerfulness under adversity

Honeysuckle for the bonds
  of love

Ivy for fidelity, friendship,
  and marriage

Linden for matrimony

Mullein for good nature

Passionflower for passion and love

Rose for love

Rose geranium for
  true friendship

Rosemary for remembrance

Sage for esteem, domestic virtue

Thyme for activity

Tulsi for protection and blessings

Valerian for an accommodat-
  ing disposition

White clover for a reminder to
  "think of me"

Begin by gathering a small bunch of herbs together, blending the base material with a few added sprigs of color and textures. This bundle will look like a tiny bouquet called a *tussie mussie*, a bouquet that is 4 to 6 inches (10–15 cm) long. Holding the bottom portion, as you would a bouquet, wire it onto your base. Continue making these small bouquets of mixed herbs and attaching them to the frame with the florist wire, layering the flowers and leaves of each one over the bottom of the previous bunch of stems. Repeat and repeat until the wreath frame is completely filled.

CHAPTER 10

My Chakra Planetary Garden

The constellations of the zodiac are of great importance for plant growth. They work through the sun, moon, and the planets, which in turn pass on their own properties to the plants through the classical elements of warmth/fire, light/air, water, and earth.

—Maria Thun

About twenty-five years ago, we had an extremely cold winter with no snow. This is a disaster for a northerner and for a northern garden. I rely on snow so I can go cross-country skiing every day (as long as the temperature is above 5°F [–15°C]). The perennials in my garden rely on snow as a blanket that keeps them safe from extreme winds and cold, and protects their roots from freezing and thawing of the soil. Repeated freezes and thaws can force the crown of a plant above the soil surface, making it even more vulnerable to extreme (possibly lethal) temperatures.

The following spring, as I expected, all the perennial plants in my garden were dead. This included rows of thyme (*Thymus vulgaris*), lavender (*Lavndula angustifolia*), and sage (*Salvia officinalis*). I was horrified at first, but then I realized the blank slate provided by the death of so many plants was an opportunity to design and plant a new formal garden. It is a wonderful moment of realization to embrace the death and rebirth process to create something new in the void.

I love formality surrounded by the soft edges of a natural landscape. The two styles complement each other very well. In fact, during my final semester of horticulture school, I completed a project on just that—blending formality with informality in gardening. I believe plants like to be played with, which is a big part of formal gardening. I think I am also partial to formal gardens because David and I met at a very formalized botanic garden, the Dallas Arboretum and Botanical Gardens.

The site where I would create my chakra garden was perfectly placed between our house and the Four Elements production fields. A formal garden was the perfect complement to our farm, honoring our love of horticulture and offering a place of beauty where we could hold educational events. Plus, the new garden would be an extensive herb collection I could stroll through to gather herbs for my morning teas, culinary herbs for dinnertime, and plants with a variety of textures and aromas for making bouquets to decorate my home. This has become my favorite path to the production fields!

This garden would also serve as a place for specimens: plants I wanted to study but wasn't yet ready to plant in a large quantity in a production field. I could study these plants, their culture, and their uses for my increased well-being or to develop into a future product.

That same spring, I was gifted a book on the chakra system for my birthday. As you may know, chakras are an Eastern system of studying the body and the energy held within each of the seven systems, rising from our roots to our higher consciousness. It blends the physical, emotional, and spiritual states of being. The cover of the book displayed a beautiful sequence of seven circles, which I immediately envisioned as the starting point of the design for my formal garden. (See the design plan on page 167.)

Designing the Garden

A garden based on the chakra system was suited perfectly for my interests in how plants assist various body systems. The garden would also be an excellent living classroom where I could teach the important connection of people to plants and the Earth as a source of health, furthering my goal to increase health for people and the Earth.

While expanding my knowledge of astrology through Kepler College classes (an online certification college named after the mathematician and astronomer Johannes Kepler), I learned that there are planets associated with each chakra. I realized that overlaying the planets onto each chakra as part of my garden design would be a fascinating project that would expand and connect my knowledge. In the 2021 season, the Chakra Planetary Garden was developed.

The garden design consists of five circular beds that represent the second through sixth chakras. The plantings for the first chakra and seventh chakra blend into the larger plantings at the two ends of the overall teaching garden area. For both versions, the Chakra Garden and the Chakra Planetary Garden, I selected planets that would represent or support each designated area. I chose plants based on their traditional uses and the color associated with each location. I selected flowering plants to provide beauty and joy throughout the garden. After all, an important feature of a garden stroll is to be surrounded by and infused with beauty.

It took three years to establish this garden, and all the right pieces came in place

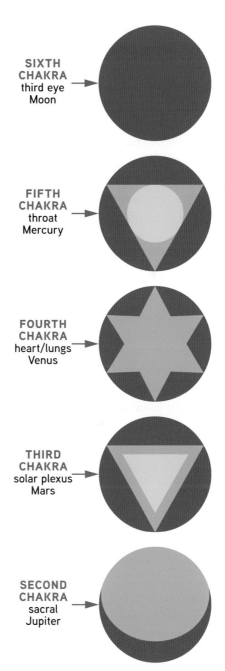

SIXTH CHAKRA
third eye
Moon

FIFTH CHAKRA
throat
Mercury

FOURTH CHAKRA
heart/lungs
Venus

THIRD CHAKRA
solar plexus
Mars

SECOND CHAKRA
sacral
Jupiter

This planting plan shows the design of the beds for the second through sixth chakras in the Planetary Chakra Garden.

at the right time. I decided I would lay pea gravel in the paths. Just at that time, a young woman applied for a job on our farm. Her work experience included hauling wheelbarrows of pea gravel in national parks in California! While she was working here, she had a dream of seven shimmering Buddhas floating over the garden, one for each chakra. For a while, we called the garden the Shimmering Buddha Garden. This garden was a wonderful educational experience for her as well.

An overlook of this garden is not like a perennial bed you would see in a garden magazine. Many of the medicinal plants have no ornamental value, but qualities exist in their constituents, or internal chemistry, that enhances and supports human metabolism. This made the flowering plants even more important, to enhance the visual engagement of the garden—the "wow" factor. My lilies and zinnias are definitely right for the job!

Students are enchanted as they enter this garden and I begin to weave the stories and traditions of the plants, which some of the visitors have known only as names they've read on the labels of herbal teas or in a journal article. I also talk about the energetic patterns of life and the systems of the body, adding information about the plants that support each system. Recently, I also began to teach about the influences of the seven planets that correspond to each chakra. People see with their own eyes and engage all the senses (this is a dramatic scratch-and-sniff aromatic garden), learning and experiencing how these life forms are intertwined.

As my lifelong study of the healing arts grows, I layer on the wisdom of various traditions, weaving these together to help visitors better understand the web of life. I have always thought studying herbs would keep me humble, because the more you learn, the more you realize you don't know. Once, when I was discussing this philosophy with 7Song, the director of the Northeast School of Botanical Medicine, he commented, "Yes, you could study just pines for a lifetime and still not know everything about *Pinus*!"

At times, my efforts to combine my understanding of planetary influences with my knowledge of the plant kingdom leaves me mystified but curious. I love studying the pieces of the puzzle, even if I can't always answer all my own questions. As I designed and developed the Chakra Garden, and as I teach others about it, my understanding deepens, of both the energies of plants and how they correspond to the body systems.

In the spirit of Nature's magic, elder planted herself front and center of the first chakra, where she happily shares space with the rugosa rose. Lower photo by Diane Lasceski-Michaels

Plants in the Chakra Planetary Garden

Chakra 7
artemisias, *Artemisia* spp.
garden angelica, *Angelica archangelica*
lamb's ears, *Stachys byzantina*
coral bells, *Heuchera* spp.

Chakra 6
tulsi, *Ocimum tenuiflorum*
rue, *Ruta graveolens*
wild lettuce, *Lactuca virosa*
valerian, *Valeriana officinalis*
wild tobacco, *Nicotiana rustica*

Chakra 5
coltsfoot, *Tussilago farfara*
elecampane, *Inula helenium*
ephedra, *Ephedra sinica*
horehound, *Marrubium vulgare*
thyme, *Thymus vulgaris*
baical, *Scutellaria baicalensis*

Chakra 4
Carefree Beauty rose, *Rosa* hybrid
lemon balm, *Melissa officinalis*
lemon verbena, *Aloysia citrodora*
balloon flower, *Platycodon grandiflorus*
lemon grass, *Cymbopogon citratus*
zinnia, *Zinnia* spp.
motherwort, *Leonurus cardiaca*
lavender, *Lavandula angustifolia*

Chakra 3
sage, *Salvia officinalis*
echinacea, *Echinacea purpurea*

dang shen, *Codonopsis pilosula*
eleuthero, *Eleutherococcus senticosus*
rhodiola, *Rhodiola* spp.
astragalus, *Astragalus* spp.
ashwagandha, *Withania somnifera*

Chakra 2

wild yam, *Dioscorea* spp.
lady's mantle, *Alchemilla vulgaris*
trumpet lily, *Lilium longiflorum*
vitex, *Vitex agnus-castus*

Chakra 1

senna, *Cassia senna*
turkey rhubarb, *Rheum officinale*
rugosa rose, *Rosa rugosa*
elder, *Sambucus canadensis*
littleleaf boxwood, *Buxus microphylla*
peony, *Paeonia* spp.

Of course, as gardens develop through the years, plants (with or without gardeners' efforts) have a way of changing the design plan, perhaps resulting in greater beauty, but perhaps causing us dismay. Have you noticed shifts in your perennial beds from year to year? Some plants expand while some seem to shrink, or they may fail to return altogether. Weeds appear, and sometimes we can welcome them for their virtues and give them a place, too.

It is always a laugh and a joy to see the wild plants move into their correct placement in the Chakra Planetary Garden, like mullein moving into the heart-lung fourth chakra. My favorite story of this plant providence comes from one spring when I was weeding to protect the red rugosa rose (*Rosa rugosa*) I had purchased specially for this garden from competition. An elderberry (*Sambucus canadensis*) had sprouted right next to the rose, and I did not like the idea of another woody perennial sharing that spot. Loving elderberry deeply, however, I could not weed it out. Later that day I realized the elder had decided to put herself in the position of the first chakra—connecting the First Chakra to the family lineage and elder! What could be more appropriate? She shares this prominent spot with the rugosa rose splendidly to this day.

The Meanings of the Chakras

Part of the mission of a garden is to experience its healing presence, like a smile and warm hug from your favorite friend, parent, or grandparent. I believe all gardens are places in which to experience healing. I have never met a garden I did not like. Could it be the colors, the beauty in the lighting or shadows, the sense of curiosity ("Who are you, beautiful plant?"), a feeling of safety, or the extra oxygen released by photosynthesizing plants, all coming together to heighten our awareness? Being in a garden creates a sense of wonder, where all your troubles disappear and your five senses open into the familiar or unknown but with a new, inspired space.

As the infinite universal wisdom would have it, overlaying the puzzle pieces of the planets into the chakras made perfect sense and fit into place. As you read the descriptions of the chakras that follow, you may want to refer to pages 170 and 171 for a plant list.

The first chakra represents our tribe, our family. The planet associated with it is Saturn, the planet of structure, rules, regulations, and

Evening, looking west over the fifth chakra, ruled by Mercury. This bed contains lung and breath herbs—elecampane, coltsfoot, ephedra, sage, thyme—and morning glories for the changeability of Mercury. Photo by Diane Lasceski-Michaels

Access to Herbal Knowledge

Correlations between plants and planets go back in history to fifteenth-century botanist and herbalist Nicholas Culpeper and earlier. Culpeper is a hero in the history of herbalism because he translated herbals from Latin to English, thus liberating the knowledge of herbal healing to the common people. I see a parallel between the situation in Culpeper's time—when common people were blocked from the knowledge that would allow them to self-diagnose and treat—and the present day in the United States, where it is illegal for unlicensed herbalists to practice and healing is approved only by undergoing certain criteria of training, similar to medical doctors, approved by the government. Plants can be much more accessible and still effective in a less clinical setting. Healing herbs are here for our benefit, just like health-promoting pure air, water, and vegetables gorgeously and generously growing from the soil.

Meanwhile, we are bombarded by advertising recommending that we *may* have a disease for which we can get a drug. This is selling disease! Fortunately, the side effects mentioned usually have a longer list than the benefits, thus deterring some from falling for this ploy.

beginnings and endings. This chakra governs our traditions, which is a first chakra and Saturnian situation.

The second chakra represents sexuality, creativity, and stepping out from the family. It is associated with Jupiter, which brings expansion, with no boundaries. Jupiter's essence is perfect for the second chakra, moving forward with no boundaries in life. It is up to us to create our life, and if you are stuck, look to see where Jupiter is in your astrological chart and how you can enhance it.

The third chakra is the solar plexus, ruled by Mars. The third chakra is where you hold your energy and power. Mars is the warrior, the one who decides what is worth fighting for and acts on it. The adaptogen herbs and immune system plants are represented here and govern which microbes the body should accept and which to reject or battle.

The fourth chakra rules our heart but also our lungs and hands. Most people could guess that the heart is ruled by Venus. Venus brings beauty and order but not fruitfulness. Herbs that support heart and lung health reside in this area of the garden. I also included plants that enrich the love/heart experience in life: roses for awe and passion, lavender for calming, lemon verbena for sending you to scent heaven (the "aaaah" factor), and rose geranium fits in this category, too. What a divine, Earthly experience to bury my face in the soft, small blankets of rose geranium foliage and breathe in the herbaceous yet floral euphoria!

The fourth chakra is in the middle. It is where we can process our intellect and inspirations from the higher chakras and blend them with our heartfelt actions, to create a world of love and beauty from our previous experiences (lower chakras) in our gardens.

The fifth chakra rules the throat, neck and shoulders, arms, and hands (which are controlled by the heart). This chakra governs sound and our creative expression, as in our voice and the messages we bring forth. Of course, Mercury, the winged messenger, rules the fifth chakra.

Table 10.1 The Meanings of the Chakras

Chakra	Keywords	Planet
First Chakra	family, fearlessness, safety, security, stability	Saturn
Second Chakra	creativity, sexual center	Jupiter
Third Chakra	personal power	Mars
Fourth Chakra	connections, heart, love	Venus
Fifth Chakra	speaking truth, verbal expression	Mercury
Sixth Chakra	inspiration, intuition, vision	Moon
Seventh Chakra	divinity, knowledge, consciousness	Sun

Mercury not only rules communication but also thought processes and ideas. I find it interesting that in our present era, most of our communications travel through air and space supported by technology, in contrast to earlier times when communication was almost all by spoken word or, later, words written on paper. What a remarkable shift from one-on-one communication to radio waves to cell phones and beyond—all this traveling invisibly through the air. This is all linked to the fifth chakra and the planet Mercury. (Look to where your Mercury is in your astrological chart to see your typical style of communication and how it can be enhanced.)

The sixth chakra is located between the eyes and is governed by the Moon. In some traditions, however, Jupiter is placed in the sixth chakra and the Moon in the second chakra (mothering, sexuality). Yes, the Moon is not a planet, it is a satellite of planet Earth; but it relays influence to us as it moves through each zodiac sign every month. I prefer the concept of the Moon residing in the sixth chakra, where we receive our intuitive messages in the area of the third eye—the gateway to higher consciousness. The Moon evokes thought and expansion, positive attributes of the sixth chakra. I love to spend time outside

Colors	Body Parts	Emotion
red (chakra) purple, blue, black (planet)	colon, lower back	To be here
orange (chakra) purple (planet)	sex organs	To feel
yellow (chakra) red (chakra)	adaptogens, balance of all systems, immune support	To act
green (chakra and planet)	heart, lungs	To love
sky blue (chakra) orange (planet)	jaw, mouth, neck, thyroid	To speak
indigo blue (chakra) white (planet)	third eye	To see
violet (chakra) gold, yellow, orange (planet)	crown, top of head	To know

Wide-leaved tussilago in the foreground is the traditional symbol for designating the home of a village herbalist.

at night gazing at the Moon, and it always evokes open, inspirational thought processes, a very sixth chakra experience.

The seventh chakra is the top of the head, symbolized by the Sun in my Chakra Planetary Garden. This pairing represents true understanding and clarity, and governs the cerebral cortex and central nervous system. Some place the planet Uranus here for its far-out, breaking-boundaries effect. I go with the Sun, though, because the seventh chakra brings the energy of enlightenment, best represented by the Sun, the star that gives all gardens and all gardeners life and the first step to enlightenment. I place sacred plants of all traditions in the seventh chakra, and I include lamb's ears (*Stachys byzantina*), evoking the energy to send and hear the chakra's messages from afar.

Students and guests experience a shift as they enter and wander through this garden. I always let people know this is a scratch-and-sniff garden and is meant to be plucked, caressed, inhaled, and inspected with all the senses.

This is just one example of using garden design to explore an area of interest. There are culinary gardens, tea gardens, medicinal gardens, clock gardens (which feature flowers that open at various times of day), Shakespearian gardens, and so many others. A garden can span hundreds of acres or dozens of inches. I love them all, and every plant contributes to our Earthly experience. Creating and utilizing my Chakra Planetary Garden has taught me and many others how beautifully and cosmically we are all—plants, people, and planets—here to support each other on this tender walk of life on Earth.

CHAPTER 11

Connecting People and Plants with Planetary Influences

We but mirror the world. All the tendencies present in the outer world are to be found in the world of our body. If we could change ourselves, the tendencies in the world would also change. As a man changes his own nature, so does the attitude of the world change toward him. This is the divine mystery supreme. A wonderful thing it is and the source of our happiness. We need not wait to see what others do.

—MAHATMA GANDHI

I've thoroughly immersed you in a gardener's view of the significance of the cycle of the Moon as it moves through the astrological signs. Now, let's step back and turn the mirror on ourselves and how astrology offers us humans a chance to polish up various aspects of our personality and open the door to living a more creative life.

In particular in this chapter, I focus on how to use your Sun sign's best attributes to serve the Earth. After all, the happiest people are those who learn to use their best qualities to serve humanity. We are given certain qualities and gifts, and we are meant to use them, like the zinnia blooms do, to bring joy.

We can use our astrological keynote as our archetype, whom we are made to be. Be the best possible by relating to this inner guide and following the open doors of the Sun and Moon signs as they move through the months. Grant Lewi, the father of modern astrology in America, referred to the Sun as indicative of "the psychological bias which will dominate your actions." He went on to say:

> You may think, dream, imagine, hope to be a thousand things, according to your Moon and your other planets: but the Sun is what you are, and to be your best self in terms of your Sun is to cause your energies to work along the path in which they will have maximum help from planetary vibrations.

I know I would love help from planetary vibrations!

This outward influence or personality with which you emulate life is what you are meant to bring to Earth. Bringing your true nature to life brings you more meaning and joy. There is a prayer whispered around the globe called "The Great Invocation" that says,

> From the centre where the Will of God is known
> Let purpose guide the little wills of men—
> The purpose which the Masters know and serve.

That means knowing your inner guidance and acting upon it. The spark that connects us all is always with us. It is up to our free will if we want to be guided by this higher internal wisdom or let our egos or any ridiculous thing like other's people's business take over.

Anyone who is passionate about plants or wants to help reclaim Nature may wonder how they can become an Earth steward. Understanding your Sun sign is a place to start.

Of course, Sun signs are just one facet of your matrix of influences and only one aspect in your astrological chart. Other influences include the planets and the houses, which represent the various aspects of life such as home, career, and relationships. These influences also include Sun signs, which potentize each area of life by the placement of planets at the moment of your birth. Think about a kaleidoscope and how, when it is turned, different patterns emerge. This is how I think of the planets imprinting personality characteristics upon each of us a little differently depending on the precise moment you arrive on Earth. They all contribute to the prism of who you are. Consider this a generalized overview of your personality that may generate a new inclination or spark that you were thinking of doing anyway.

Observing life as it runs through people, plants, and planets gives a more inclusive view of how we are all connected. From this vantage point, it becomes more difficult to separate our actions from everything else. It becomes easier to navigate a reality where we are all in this together—here to help and support each other. Many in a capitalist society have realized that working to accumulate things is superficial compared to what we can create and contribute as we try to leave the world a better place. The breakdown of each astrological sign, or personality type, illuminates qualities that are there to serve us all, therefore bringing true light, love, and joy to life.

As a new horticulture graduate with an inclination toward herbs, I wondered how I could contribute to regenerating the abused and ignored attitude toward Earth and herbalism. An inquisitive student of gardening or plants can look closely at their astrological chart to fine-tune their best qualities. Many of the careers I mention in this chapter could also be avocations to uplift your life. I don't mean to suggest that

Dates for Each Sun Sign

Aries	March 21–April 19
Taurus	April 20–May 20
Gemini	May 21–June 20
Cancer	June 21–July 22
Leo	July 23–August 22
Virgo	August 23–September 22
Libra	September 23–October 22
Scorpio	October 23–November 21
Sagittarius	November 22–December 21
Capricorn	December 22–January 19
Aquarius	January 20–February 18
Pisces	February 19–March 20

everything I mention below leads to a sustainable lifestyle. However, I believe it will increase your joy.

To gather more guidance on how to contribute to a better world through the insights of astrology, generate a free chart online. A popular site is www.astro.com. You will need to know your birth time, date, and place of birth.

The place to look for your vocational inclinations is at the midpoints that correspond to north, south, east, and west, as if the zodiac wheel were a compass. These are the horizon points and the axis points at the top and bottom of the chart. The tenth house has to do with your career. Look to see if any planets are located in that section for insights. The sixth house has to do with employment.

Table 11.1 The Archetypes of the Ruling Planets

Name	Archetypes	Associated Zodiac Signs
Sun	self-expression, self-confidence, the self	Leo
Moon	caring and showing concern for others, emotional disposition, intuition	Cancer
Mercury	the winged messenger, language and communication skills, the mind, thoughts and words	Gemini, Virgo
Venus	love and beauty, our passions, possessions, people we love	Taurus, Libra
Mars	the warrior, abundant energy, drive, initiative, courage and motivation	Aries, Scorpio
Jupiter	everything expansive, jovial, moments of opportunity, enjoying the journey	Sagittarius, Pisces
Saturn	boundaries, focus, commitment, hard work, discrimination, organization	Capricorn, Aquarius
Uranus	surprises, eccentricity, rebellion, electricity, innovation	Aquarius
Neptune	new, shiny, uncertain, the ocean	Pisces
Pluto	subconscious fear, intense, eruptive, certain change, dissolve boundaries, divine potential	Scorpio

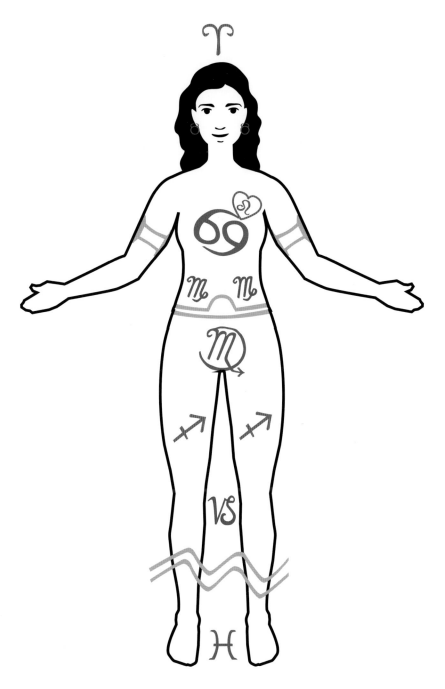

The zodiac woman shows the seat of each of the astrological signs in the body.
Illustration by Jerry Chapa

Know that fame and wealth are not always the outcome of a successful career or avocation. What brings joy is following our inner, individual truth. That is what I could call real success. My hope is that all of us can pitch in and create a more beautiful world for all species in our gardens and communities.

Up to this chapter, I have focused primarily on the Moon's influence on plants and garden activity. But in this chapter, I explore the implications of Sun signs on the *gardeners*, because your Sun sign rules your personality.

Each zodiac sign has a ruling planet, as shown in Table 11.1. This influences the personality of the sign. Take Mars, for example. Mars implies strength and power, key aspects of both Aries and Scorpio, which are associated with Mars. Venus implies beauty and charm, key aspects of Taurus and Libra. Following these astral guides, you gain a better understanding of what each sign reveals about your personality and life.

Each sign description in this chapter lists the guiding element that governs that sign. I also list the modality of the sign. Is that sign a cardinal sign (an initiator); is it fixed and trustworthy to carry a project to fruition; or is it mutable and flexible in some way? Key concepts describe the energy of the sign in a few words. Each sign rules a particular place in the body, and I list that as well.

The suggested herbs for balance are very generalized, pertaining to the iconic astrological sign. No one is really a cookie-cutter version of a sign, because of all the other influences that imprint on a human: astrological, physical, mental, and emotional. After all, who has met different people with the same personality even once?

The project proposition for each sign is a generalized guide to spark the inspiration in you to act with your natural talents. Following that is the sign's best gardening activities and then archetypal advice, which you can think of as finding your teacher after a lifelong search. Find your sign's ruling planet in your astrological chart and decipher the message by its house placement. Each house holds an aspect of life, like home, family, career, education, resources, and so on. This concept becomes clearer when you find your chart online. You find that figure and are guided with some simple but profound advice. "Get going!" (says the Aries).

Aries ♈ *The Ram*

Dates: March 21–April 19

Planet: Mars

Element: Fire

Modality: cardinal

Key concepts: courage, enthusiasm, a pioneer

Key phrase: I am.

Associated body parts: face, head, motor centers of the brain, upper jaw

Herbs for balance: cooling roots and yin tonics, such as peony (*Paeonia* spp.) root; nervines such as lemon balm (*Melissa officinalis*) or skullcap (*Scutellaria lateriflora*)

Aries, the first sign of the zodiac, begins with the first day of spring. The glyph represents the ram's horns or the Fountain of Life. Aries is a cardinal Fire sign. Use this energy to begin projects. Starting something new on your own fits with the strong self-identity of Aries. Aries is a trailblazer.

I use my dynamic Aries energy to start thousands of herb transplants every year and plant them in the fields to cultivate, harvest, and use in my Four Elements herbal products. When I began my business in 1987, I had no idea how much work it would create for me and others as the business grew over time. The enthusiasm of an Aries is unstoppable.

Aries is ruled by the planet Mars, and like Mars the Greek god of war, Aries takes focused and direct action. The ram can be aggressive not out of meanness but because it just needs to get where it is going.

Although Aries likes being the leader, they need some helpers to complete projects and attend to details. Being a double Aries, I can speak to this reality. My vision was to develop a farm-based business. I wanted to work with plants and be outdoors. My system was to envision the goal, then take a step toward it every day. I left the city of my high school the day I graduated and moved to Madison to begin my degree in horticulture at the University of Wisconsin–Madison. As the years went by, I founded my business and moved it forward one step at a time. After twenty years, things were becoming complicated as my "mini-empire" expanded. I had a greenhouse where I started transplants, production fields to organically grow herbs for the products, an

The warmth and energy of this dahlia reflects the spirits of Aries and Leo.

apothecary, staff manufacturing the products, an office manager, and a few other employees. Managing all of this was getting out of hand.

Then the FDA showed up to look for any dirt between tables or wording on my product labels describing the benefits of herbs that crossed the structure–function line. (FDA rules state that, if you manufacture herbal products, you cannot claim that these herbs treat, mitigate, or heal, even if you are speaking of traditional knowledge.) That visit was a turning point. I realized a lot of protocols should be put in place, and I needed the right people to manage this—not me. Extensive details make me uneasy. According to my sister, I don't even see details. It's true! Think of a ram climbing a mountain. The goal is reaching the top, not looking at the scenery along the way. It wasn't until one day as I was nearing age sixty, I stopped, out of breath, and thought, "Could I take a break and look at what I've created, breathe it in, and feel appreciation?"

In recent years, the annual inspection by my organic certifier has become nearly as scary as a visit from the FDA, because the number of details organic growers are being required to attend to is beyond my capacity. Thank goodness, Gaia has now brought the perfect employee to Four Elements Organic Herbals to manage this aspect of the business. (Thank you, Liz!) I am extremely grateful for her.

Aries can bring visions into tangible matter, but things can get messy without teamwork. Because Aries are visionaries who can see so well where they want a project to end up, they may take off without a plan. That might work out well because the plan can be figured out as you go. And as we all know, circumstances in life can change fast, so having the vision to keep going may be more important than knowing the details. I have had to morph my plans in more ways than I can imagine in response to changing weather patterns, changing markets, and changes in the qualities and moods of the staff. The fiery Aries energy sparks progress to unite labor and matter to manifest achievement. Aries is a warrior against limitations.

Look for an Aries to initiate and persevere. In service and creative action, beauty radiates and creates joy in an Aries world.

Project propositions: Aries's pioneering spirit can begin large projects that require physical strength, like starting an organic farm or a garden-based company, as long as they are in charge and can express their individuality.

A greenhouse business focused on springtime sales would be enjoyable because growing transplants requires many beginnings, but then you can sell these young plants to others who can cultivate and maintain them.

Another great project for Aries is to create urban gardens. Activist citizens in challenged urban neighborhoods are planting vegetable, herb, and flower gardens in vacant lots that can engage and enliven communities. The urgent need for gardens in food deserts is critical and needs addressing now.

In general, just plant seeds.

On a smaller scale, Aries could develop a school project teaching children about gardening.

For an Aries enterprise to be truly successful, people with different qualities can help lead the project. What may be lacking in Aries is attention to detail, contemplative thinking, and a smooth negotiating style—Aries are assertive! Through Aries's efforts and vision, they can create a harmoniously united organization.

Best gardening activities: Harvest (I have often said I was born to pick things) and prune. Control insects and pests. Cultivate, plow, and weed.

Archetypal advice from an Aries: What motivates you? Look to your Mars.

Taurus ☉ *The Bull or Cow*

Dates: April 20–May 20
Planet: Venus
Element: Earth

Modality: fixed
Key concepts: creative, realistic, stable, strong
Key phrase: I have.
Associated body parts: chin, ears, neck, throat, tongue
Herbs for balance: burdock (*Arctium lappa*), dandelion,
   yellow dock (*Rumex crispus*) roots

The spring seeds of Aries germinate into Taurus, the mothering sign. Taurus is the energy of nurturing, often represented by a bull but with the energy of the mothering cow. This Earth sign nurtures growth and a movement within toward perfection, or our higher goals. Like good parents, Taurus sees a divine purpose and plan, and creates better solutions to problems by accessing the inner guide, not just relying on a forceful personality.

Did you ever watch a zinnia seed spring out of the ground, accessing resources to bloom a vibrant color? Zinnias are destined to bring smiles to our inner core, supported by the energy of Taurus to bring forth our best selves.

Gardening would be a perfect pastime for a Taurus. This could be growing food for increased health, acquiring land for beauty and security, or gardening for aesthetics in their surroundings. They are motivated by purpose. Earthy and stable, they will be there to tend to all stages of development. Taurus loves their homes and stability. They are motivated by purpose and want to manifest something tangible in their life.

Grounded Taurus pursues and manifests a constructive life, which is how to unlock one of the secrets to happiness. Governed by Venus, they bring people together to increase love and beauty, and can lead the world to a new level of harmony, if that is their goal. They are known to be possessive, but this comes from concentrating on productivity. Count on a Taurus to set new and higher goals, to make new plans to meet those goals, bringing the spirit of unification and order. As the Gemini can figure out how to make things work, the Taurus can find the right tools.

Project propositions: This fixed Earth sign can bring an idea or project
   into creative manifestation. They bring harmony and beauty into
   the project. Their stubborn nature and desire for creativity are

assets toward making things happen. Tauruses are good people managers and they can help projects that involve conflict resolution. Their unique quality is to bridge humanity and divinity, and throw light on the path. They bring out inner guidance that leads to harmony and creative solutions. Taurus is down-to-Earth and pragmatic. Farming or any vocation related to environmental work, such as preserving wetlands or green space, would be suitable. That pragmatic approach could serve in the accounting or finance of a proposed venture. On a backyard scale, Taurus lights the way, so you could install lighting to feature the beauty in your garden.

(It is the light that opens the eyes.)

Best gardening activities: Plant seeds. Organize a garden or landscape, and the people involved in the project. Transplant or graft trees, which is also favored.

Archetypal advice from a Taurus: What is the best solution for all involved? Look to your Venus.

Gemini ♊ *The Twins*

Dates: May 21–June 20

Planet: Mercury

Element: Air

Modality: mutable

Key concepts: communication, curiosity, intelligence

Key phrase: I think.

Associated body parts: arms, hands, hearing, lungs, nerves, shoulders, speech

Herbs for balance: elecampane (*Inula helenium*), mullein (*Verbascum thapsus*), lobelia (*Lobelia inflata*), skullcap (*Scuttelaria lateriflora*)

At germination, a seedling sends roots down, looking for water and nutrients. Then the shoot extends upward and reaches for the sun. Leaves begin to photosynthesize, and occasionally the top of the plant grows too fast before the roots can stabilize. This dichotomy represents Gemini, or the Twins. The instability of Gemini produces a decision toward the right choice, by considering both options. A Gemini can help with decision-making and can be a good manager.

Gemini shows its airy and mutable quality by being an excellent, but sometimes verbose, communicator. Communication moves through the air, and Gemini is there to capture it. If your community needs a spokesperson for developing community gardens, conserving safe habitats for birds and pollinators, eliminating herbicides and pesticides in common spaces, or seed sovereignty, ask a Gemini to step up and communicate the urgency to leaders who need that education.

The sign of the Twins sees and displays duality. Watch a Gemini problem solve and evoke goodwill while making decisions using mental and emotional qualities. They have the power to discriminate and choose with active intelligence. In fact, I say that David, my Gemini, gardens like Rembrandt, with perfect lines and forms, keenly discriminating which plant stays or goes. Whereas being Aries, I garden like Monet, with flowing lines of beloved medicinal weeds growing freely amongst my crops. Together we have created a horticultural masterpiece!

Project propositions: A ravenous researcher and data gatherer, Gemini's thought process can get to the bottom of designing a project, keeping all the necessary data. Before the internet, my Gemini husband would buy newspapers from both coasts before buying new stereo equipment, studying quality and pricing. Now, with YouTube video tutorials to guide him, there is nothing in our house that David cannot fix. Ask him anything about any tree or shrub in his collection at the University of Wisconsin–Madison Arboretum: he might begin by relating the details of the plant explorer who brought the plant to this country. A Gemini makes a great curator of a collection!

A job that offers variety and stimulation would suit a Gemini. Information gathering, writing, and anything emphasizing language, communication, and research would make a Gemini feel in their place. A Gemini mind is intellectual and can gather experience and concepts together, then interpret and classify them. Be aware: these outcomes are guided by cultural norms and rationality. They may get stuck believing only what they want to believe and never understand another point of view.

Best gardening activities: Gemini rules the arms, so harvesting is a good job for them. (Even though most Moon gardeners wait for the harvest days to receive what they earned from their efforts, a

Call on a Gemini when it's time to harvest a big crop of mint! Their quick hands and arms will help the job move along faster.

Gemini may be more efficient at this chore.) A Gemini will also work hard to achieve a fruitful harvest season. The airy quality supports effective weeding, cultivation, and insect control. David's gardens are beautifully tidy!

Archetypal advice from a Gemini: How do you want to communicate your vision? Look to your Mercury.

Cancer ♋ *The Crab*

Dates: June 21–July 22
Planet: Moon
Element: Water
Modality: cardinal
Key concepts: empathy, nurture, reassurance
Key phrase: I feel.
Associated body parts: chest, ribs, stomach, temperature regulation
Herbs for balance: adaptogens (for managing stress) such as ashwagandha (*Withania somnifera*), eleuthero (*Acanthopanax senticosus*), lemon balm (*Melissa officinalis*)

Aries is the germinating seed; roots form and secure it to Earth in Taurus; Gemini distinguishes the duality of life. Then Cancer condenses the Air and proceeds to discover the depth and range of emotions of being alive—they are profoundly feeling beings, ruled by the emotional Moon.

Cancer aligns with the Sun at the summer solstice. The Sun reaches its longest day and shortest night, and then the nights begin to lengthen, giving strength to nocturnal, feminine Cancer. Because Cancer brings in a season and is a cardinal sign, they are initiators and take action, but they operate on the sensory level, reflecting a feminine and nocturnal quality. The consciousness of Mother Earth is in their awareness, and this state of consciousness can be considered where they reside—their home. Holding the consciousness like Water, Cancer is less likely to fall to self-deception, especially when governed by higher spiritual goals. As Dane Rudhyar, one of the most respected astrologers of the twentieth century, wrote:

> As the mind attempts to interpret the messages it receives and to deduce from them—without allowing itself to be self-deceived—guiding lines in the pursuit of ever-higher, more encompassing goal[s], the quality of non-possessiveness is also necessary; for in order to be truly open and sensitive, one has to be positive and secure, yet non-attached to past experiences.

Cancer is governed by the Moon, the most mothering of signs. When functioning on a higher level, Cancer knows we are all connected and senses the truth that helping others and feeling their needs helps them as well.

Cancer avoids confrontation and tends to sidestep and back away like the crab, consciously choosing peace. When confronted by difficulties, they may want a warm blanket in a cozy spot to soothe and protect them, like the shield of the crab.

Transitioning between Air and Water can be a jarring effect, but in order to experience life, we need a full range of Water-ruled emotions. The spirit of life can now shine under this influence and inspire consciousness for improving and moving cultures forward.

Project propositions: A Cancer appreciates their home: "I build a lighted house and therein I dwell." Engaging the beauty of writing or photography in gardens and expressing the comfort therein would be a good use of Cancer energy. Anything nurturing or caring, such as organizing farm- or garden-to-table meals or creating activities for healing and nurturing in the garden, would be beneficial.

Organizing a retreat for local Reiki practitioners or creating pollinator gardens would serve Gaia well. I think of my daughter, who is a Cancer, as a dragonfly or butterfly, always keeping the peace and creating a sense of light-hearted joy. An architect or designer in this category could create very comfortable surroundings that would nurture and support humanity's environment.

Best gardening activities: Cancer is the best sign for planting seeds. Planting anything would be a good choice for a Cancer. That might include being a messenger, planting the right idea in the minds of others. The nurturing and empathetic quality of this Moon-influenced sign could be well suited to organizing vegetable and flower distribution for the underserved.

Archetypal advice from a Cancer: What do you need to feel comfortable and elevated in life? Look to your Moon.

Leo ♌ *The Lion*

Dates: July 23–August 22
Planet: Sun
Element: Fire
Modality: fixed
Key concepts: individuality, love, a strong will, warmth
Key phrase: I will.
Associated body parts: the back, heart, sensory nerves, spine
Herbs for balance: chamomile (*Matricaria chamomilla*), passionflower (*Passiflora* spp.), St. John's wort (*Hypericum perforatum*), violets (*Viola* spp.)

When Leo aligns with the Sun in August, gardens have gathered the summer sunshine and are gloriously displaying their unique expression. Harvests are ready in full fruition. Representing the abundance of summer, Sunny Leo is considered a potent, actualized being who can maintain and sustain projects or systems that are already in motion. One of my Leo friends, Laurel, carries on the tradition of acupuncture. Her work comes from the heart, comforting her patients with her sunny disposition. Leos want to control their own destiny. A drive for self-expression and authenticity abound, making this a very creative sign.

Leo is a fixed sign, features group relations, and has a stabilizing effect. They like to lead groups into action. Heart-centered Leo shows that love is the guiding principle of all human relations. Their consciousness of individuality is an inspiration for others to improve.

Look to a sunny Leo when creating bold gardens or community gardens, or when offering garden tours.

Project propositions: Choose Leo as a natural leader who enjoys working with groups (as long as they are the director or manager of the organization). Their upbeat creativity will make the project shine. Public projects would benefit from a Leo leader because they project charisma and warmth, with a bit of dramatic flair. Children would benefit from learning from a Leo instructor, so volunteering for gardening programs at schools would be well suited. For several years, I visited our local elementary school to plant zinnias and sunflowers with the children so they could bring them home at Mother's Day to plant outdoors in the ground or in a pot. What a joy to watch these youths witness the wonders held in a seed. Teaching in community colleges, local events, or even cooking classes featuring medicinal/culinary herbs would be an asset to any community.

Best gardening activities: A warm and sunny Leo personality attracts and inspires others. Put them in charge of an organization for public gardens, including schools, arboreta, or community gardens

Echinacea is a balancing herb for a Virgo.

to generate interest and to intrigue newcomers into joining the organization. This charismatic person could be good at generating funds, too.

Archetypal advice from a Leo: You are already guided by the Sun, so where can you utilize this bright energy?

Virgo ♍ *The Virgin*

Dates: August 23–September 22
Planet: Mercury
Element: Earth
Modality: mutable
Key concepts: creation of beauty, nurturing, precision, efficiency
Key phrase: I analyze.
Associated body parts: diaphragm, immune system, intestines, joints, nervous system, pancreas, solar plexus
Herbs for balance: nervines (soothing nervous excitement) such as lemon balm (*Melissa officinalis*), valerian (*Valeriana officinalis*), astragalus (*Astragalus* spp.), echinacea (*Echinacea* spp.)

Although Virgo is an Earth sign, it is not used for fruitfulness. After all, she represents the Virgin, or the self-assured single woman. The mutable quality means that Virgo may carry some of the features of the sign that follows, the Air of Libra. This is one of the joys of studying Nature: anomalies to look for and discover. It is a reason I love to learn from Nature, although for some, like Virgos, putting things into formulas resonates and describes things more tangibly.

Purity is a word used to describe Virgo. Think of pure water, which has no other particles in it, solely hydrogen and oxygen. Constant reaching for perfection can create such purity. Virgo has discernment. Pure reason, thinking, pure expression of unity, harmony, dedication to human welfare, total commitment to serve, invincible striving toward perfection. The true sense of the word discrimination—meaning the quality or power of finely distinguishing between two alternatives, not against a person or class—is expertly presented in this sign. One of the best features of this sign is that Virgos will use their discernment to see through popularly held beliefs and speak their truth through deep

Creating a serene garden for contemplation would be a satisfying choice for a Virgo. Photo by Diane Lasceski-Michaels

reflection. This can help to break down barriers and to see the truth when convention does not hold up.

On the downside, Virgo's attention to detail can send them down the rabbit hole of never-ending perfection. But the ideal of perfection that Virgo strives for connects matter and spirit. Spirit appropriates matter, then matter strives to manifest the power, beauty, and mystery of spirit. When these come together in harmony, the result is beauty, and a Virgo has the power to manifest this truth.

Virgo has the universal urge to serve and to make things beautiful. These connoisseurs stand to harmonize and create greatness. By serving the virtue of beauty, they inspire, nourish, and reveal this human need for beauty.

Virgo rules the tools and techniques we use to deal with day-to-day life.

Project propositions: A Virgo is well placed in a job that needs attention to detail and to create beauty. (It is recommended to set your dentist appointments during a Virgo Moon: for beauty and precision straightening of your teeth, eyeing the details, and creating beautiful smiles.)

Virgo could create beautiful garden designs with accurate architectural drawings. They would understand the best uses of color, form, and an overview. Ruled by Mercury, they are good messengers of communication and could help sell a design project. Their keen vision of details would serve them well in an editor position, fine-tuning gardening books and articles.

Best gardening activities: Setting up commercial kitchens for quality production to create herbal medicine would benefit from the skills of Virgo. Count on a Virgo-designed garden to be stunningly beautiful and hold space for people to be in the wonder and glory of Nature. Working in any gardening publication would utilize their skill of details and the communication skills of Mercury, the winged messenger.

Archetypal advice from a Virgo: What is the ultimate beauty that you can create, and how will you communicate that message? Look to your Mercury for guidance.

Libra ♎ *The Scales*

Dates: September 23–October 22
Planet: Venus
Element: Air
Modality: cardinal
Key concepts: adaptability, balance, fairness
Key phrase: I balance.
Associated body parts: hormonal and chemical balance, kidneys, lumbar region of back
Herbs for balance: cornsilk, dandelion, vitex (*Vitex agnus-castus*), wild yam (*Dioscorea* spp.)

Libra begins with the autumnal equinox, as the Sun crosses the equator, heading south from the Northern Hemisphere. The focus turns from the individual (Aries through Virgo) to group consciousness. Libra begins this group-focused cycle featuring one-on-one relationships, and this cycle ends with Pisces extending this otherness to a mystic oneness with the universe.

Libras like people, and they are devoted to the growth of society. This devotion comes through with the element of Air, communicating with harmony and consideration for the listener, often attending more to the other's thoughts and stories and acting as a sounding board, then offering guidance when asked. The cardinal aspect of Libra is in taking control through this strategy of serving others.

Libra symbolizes peace and beauty perhaps better than any. They love with care and concern for the other. Dane Rudhyar described a Libra as showing:

> . . . "equanimity in love"—love which is deeply peaceful, serene, which requires no passionate responses, which remains love even if seeming indifference or neglect is the response, which is truly a gift, a sharing of what one IS far more than what one HAS.

We think of Libra as being balanced, but it's important to understand that balance can be a kind of striving: once we reach equilibrium, Libras don't just stop and stagnate. We must then see the next goal and seek to achieve that. Equilibrium is not the goal but a means to perpetuate motion forward. The planets themselves demonstrate this concept of balance: they are held in place in their individual orbits through a combination of attraction and repulsion, and overall, within that balance, they keep moving onward.

This dichotomy plays out as a good time for planting, and flowers are recommended to be planted under this sign. It is considered semi-fruitful. Other features of this sign are extreme care in detail. They level the path toward perfection by balancing spirit with matter, abstract thinking with scientific thinking, idealism with practicality. This balance can help with pollution, knowing that outer pollution may be coming from our inner pollution, the law of "As above, so below."

Project propositions: Create spaces of peace, harmony, and beauty through gardens and landscapes, perhaps advocating for the underserved through your work. A Libra uses their law of harmony to fine-tune color, form, movement, and sound. Interdependence in organizing with another for a community project would likely succeed, such as working with an artist to co-organize an installation in a park or arboretum. Libras would make great consultants, fundraisers for public gardens, or environmental attorneys.

Wild yam is a balancing herb for a Libra. Photo by Diane Lasceski-Michaels

Best gardening activities: Plant flowers. Create bouquets to bring gardens indoors and brighten the world.

Archetypal advice from a Libra: How can you help build human cooperation to improve the health of people and the planet? Look to your Venus for guidance.

Scorpio ♏ *The Scorpion*

Dates: October 23–November 21
Planets: Mars, Pluto
Element: Water
Modality: fixed
Key concepts: control, details, efficiency, intensity
Key phrase: I want.
Associated body parts: elimination organs, reproductive organs, sacrum, sweat glands
Herbs for balance: crampbark (*Viburnum opulus*), ginger (*Zingiber officinale*), ginseng (*Panax ginseng*), raspberry leaf, sage (*Salvia officinalis*)

The time of Scorpio is a time of dormancy and holding energy inward. Everything the summer Sun has shone on them has been distilled and held within. In many parts of the Northern Hemisphere, the soil is starting to freeze and perennials are fully withdrawn, holding energy in their roots. This is reflective of inward-focused Scorpio.

This inward-contemplative sign holds the willpower that creates efficiency in reaching their goals. Resourceful Scorpio can be an agent for change through their deep thinking and problem-solving capabilities that can penetrate to the core of the problem. They have the confidence to put faith in their own resources and to process ideas toward discerning the best choice. A Scorpio can propose direct solutions if given the needed time to themselves.

Deep thought and strategizing can overcome Earthly obstacles. By directing focus on biological and psychological forces, they can withstand the shadow side with their strong willpower, if they choose. A warning to Scorpio: your competitive nature may miss the mark by thinking that "success" rather than the experience is the goal. The *dedication* to the goal, however, is more important than the result in a life based on truth.

Scorpio, representing the autumn, watches everything die, and, by accepting this inevitability of mortality, finds the beauty and richness of every sacred moment of life. Think of rich compost that comes from last year's vines, which were once full of fruit but now can rejuvenate and help create the cycle again.

Project propositions: Using their keen sense of detail for completing and implementing details for organic certification or other regulatory paperwork would be work well suited to a Scorpio. Likewise, a laboratory job analyzing the chemical composition of soil or the chemical constituents in herbs could be a good fit. Solo activities suit Scorpios because they get what they want. Their penchant for investigation, deep thought, and understanding could be applied to editing gardening publications or any type of horticultural research project. They are typically interested in the mysteries of life and in healing practices, and should grow medicinal and culinary herbs, for their own use or for others. A Scorpio should have a compost pile or organize a community composting system because regeneration of life and death is under Scorpio's rule.

Best gardening activities: Plant, transplant, or graft using the fixed Water element that the Scorpio carries. Set up, maintain, and utilize compost heaps, promoting the regeneration process that will help to improve next year's gardens.

Archetypal advice from a Scorpio: How will you use your willpower to achieve the greater good? Look to your Pluto to see what is out of balance in this world and visualize the best breakthrough for all involved.

Sagittarius ♐ *The Archer*

Dates: November 22–December 21
Planet: Jupiter
Element: Fire
Modality: mutable
Key concepts: activity, generosity, idealism

Key phrase: I see.

Associated body parts: central nervous system, hips, liver, thighs

Herbs for balance: berberine-rich plants such as barberry (*Berberis vulgaris*) root, goldenseal (*Hydrastis canadensis*), Oregon grape (*Berberis aquifolium*) root; black cohosh (*Actaea racemosa*); wild lettuce (*Lactuca virosa*)

The Fire signs in general, but Sagittarius especially, would be great for conducting garden tours or outings for connecting people to the out-of-doors. Their sense of wonder and enthusiasm inspires others. A Sagittarius is curious and wants to explore and discover the mysteries in life and Nature.

"I see the goal, reach it, then see another," is the thought process of a Sagittarius. They have high levels of awareness. This motivation invokes striving, idealism, and a sense of direction, leading them to their destination.

Project propositions: Playful Sagittarius would be in a good position to connect children to gardens or as a guide to take groups out camping in Nature. (It is always recommended to go camping under a Sagittarius Moon.) A curious Sagittarius might study the influence of medicinal wild plants and their uses, research the status of songbirds and pollinators, shining a light on the intrinsic place in the web of life.

Best gardening activities: Harvesting and pruning are recommended for the enthusiastic Sagittarius. Other activities include controlling insects and pests, plowing, and weeding.

Archetypal advice from a Sagittarius: How can your goals become more inclusive to expand and capture new ideas to find abundance? Look to your Jupiter.

Capricorn ♑ *The Goat, or Goat-Fish*

Dates: December 22–January 19
Planet: Saturn
Element: Earth

Modality: cardinal

Key phrase: I use.

Key concepts: aspiration, power, practicality, responsibility

Associated body parts: bones, knees, skin

Herbs for balance: blue vervain (*Verbena hastata*), calendula (*Calendula officinalis*), chamomile (*Matricaria chamomilla*), horsetail (*Equisetum* spp.), lemon balm (*Melissa officinalis*)

Capricorns will succeed. Step by step, these Earthy people bring their labor to fruition. Any garden projects that require patience, determination, and hard work, such as converting a conventional farm to organic, could succeed here.

Capricorns are concerned with economics, distribution of money, and seeds, including the vision of Illumination. They bring prosperity, abundance, new ideas, new visions, and new viewpoints. Think of the vantage point of the goat standing high up on the mountain.

A Capricorn uses their light to serve humanity, has strong will, and can fight limitations.

Growing and selling herbs could be a good fit for an outgoing personality like an Aries (me) or for a Capricorn. Photo courtesy of Regina Flanigan

Project propositions: Capricorns strive for achievement with authority and security. They have a sense of trust in the human spirit to work toward what ultimately ties us to a bigger picture. Positions involving management, responsibility, respect, and recognition will be carried out with determination by a Capricorn. They can handle big jobs with their grounded, Earthy spirit.

Best gardening activities: Anything related to farms and farming could suit a Capricorn. They like structure and can organize and lead well. I recommend working with organic farming in a leadership role.

Archetypal advice from a Capricorn: How can you use your focus to accomplish your vision? Look to your Saturn for structure.

Aquarius ♒ *The Water Bearer*

Dates: January 20–February 18
Planets: Saturn, Uranus
Element: Air
Modality: fixed
Key concepts: Knowledge, humanity, love, innovation
Key phrase: I love.
Associated body parts: ankles, lower leg, veins, the electrical system in the body, circulation
Herbs for balance: chamomile (*Matricaria chamomilla*), kava kava (*Piper methysticum*), passionflower (*Passiflora* spp.), skullcap (*Scutellaria lateriflora*), valerian (*Valeriana officinalis*)

Advocating for any fair agricultural or beautifying project would be well served by an Aquarian. Aquarius will seek the perfection of society through communication with group consciousness. Their sense of vision could be applied to advocating for large-scale causes such as combating climate change or phasing out the use of agricultural chemicals. They have the viewpoint of group consciousness, and can find opportunities for unification, an admirable virtue. They are great connectors.

Aquarius is about change. They have the spirit (Fire), physical (Earth), mental (Air), and emotional (Water) resources to manifest desires.

Living in Nature would suit them, because they are the sign that is most susceptible to electromagnetic fields, which are more prevalent in cities.

Project propositions: Advocating for any fair agricultural or beautifying project would be well served by an Aquarius. An activist or lobbyist for humanitarian causes or conservation of Nature would benefit from the electrical energy of Aquarius: greater levels of awareness, and the attraction to them of receptive and sensitive people They do this with a commanding energy and a sense of personhood.

Best gardening activities: Harvest, plow, and weed. Control insects and pests. Due to their electrical and erratic energy, they may like the rhythm of agriculture with its variation between demanding times and down times.

Archetypal advice from an Aquarius: How can you reinvent yourself? Look to the placement of your Uranus for new ideas and inventions regarding ways to break through social norms.

Pisces ♓ *The Fishes*

Dates: February 19–March 20
Planet: Jupiter, Neptune
Element: Water
Modality: mutable
Key concepts: adaptability, faith in the future, sensitivity, vulnerability
Key phrase: I believe.
Associated body parts: feet, lymphatic system
Herbs for balance: astragalus (*Astragalus* spp.), echinacea (*Echinacea* spp.), mugwort (*Artemisia vulgaris*), oat (*Avena sativa*) straw, sage (*Salvia officinalis*), skullcap (*Scutellaria lateriflora*)

Pisces is a deep and thoughtful individual with a focus on spirituality, mysticism, and human services. Pisces's career could include projects that require faith, trust, and compassion. Perhaps learning about herbal wellness, they could join a nonprofit organization that provides help in troubled zones, such as Herbalists Without Borders.

Their sensitive nature could connect them with pollinators, birds, and especially the plight of fish, with Pisces' watery nature. In January 2023, the Environmental Working Group published a report explaining that virtually all fish are contaminated with mercury, perfluoroalkyl and polyfluoroalkyl substances (PFASs), polychlorinated biphenyls (PCBs), dioxins, and pesticide residues. When I was a college student taking chemistry in the mid-1970s, we were taught that fish were especially vulnerable to toxins. These substances build up with each generation of fish and do not degrade or go away. I almost jumped out of my seat! We should stop this today! (Why was I the only one looking so disturbed?) Fish are a major food source. And let's consider how much we need healthy water for all living things. We are in a closed system. But, the corruption of fish and more has gotten worse and people are finally noticing. Pisces, how can we be a part of the solution? *By being the best example we can be*, given our circumstances.

Project propositions: These deep individuals could run retreats connecting people to the natural environment, offering a deep, transformative experience. They have an urge to serve and preserve, so they could contribute their sensitive natures to organizations that help preserve environments.

Best gardening activities: Join in groups with a large vision to unite people over unseen things, such as pollution or visionary quests that protect nature and the environment.

Archetypal advice from a Pisces: How can you help to build a new common philosophy based on essential and universal dignity for all life forms? Look to your Neptune for your hidden powers.

A Celestial Perspective

Some gardeners tell me that they shy away from following celestial gardening practices because they're afraid they can't keep up with the requirements of the schedule. I tell them, "Don't worry. Nature is forgiving!" Like my friend Lisa says, "I am a gardening-by-the-weekend gardener." She tends her garden with love and care as her schedule allows, and her garden still provides her with lots of delicious vegetables to eat. So don't worry about following the signs every day in every way. There will be times when an astrological gardening scheme does not fit into your life, because of either weather or your schedule, and there's no requirement to follow all the guidelines outlined in this book.

What Matters Most

Linking the planets to the plants is a lens that reveals a much bigger orchestra than is commonly perceived or respected in our Western culture. At a time when so many people have been trained to see division instead of unity, the practice of observing the cords that tie the universal energy together creates a sense of peace and acceptance. I have learned to observe rhythms, that there is a time to sow and a time to reap. There are dry times and wet times. One supports the other in the big picture. Instead of just seeing duality—right and wrong, left and right—I see a big wheel with the spokes and hub moving through time and space. In this view, we can breathe deeper and take our place in the cosmic dance of life, accepting less stress and more joy and ease.

Instead of reading the news about "us versus them," we could study the links between people, plants, and planets in this wondrous web of life. What a choice to make, and what a relief!

The most urgent message from Nature that we need to pay attention to is that we are all connected on this planet. Earth is a closed system. If we spray poisons that kill insects by messing with their nervous systems, we should not be surprised if we see increased rates of Parkinson's disease (according to the National Institute of Health). Increasingly, more people are realizing that our societal disconnection with Nature is leading to such dire impacts on human health. They are hearing Nature's resounding response: "Pay attention!"

When I am looking for answers on a deeper level, I turn to Nature. In silence and with patience, clarity always comes. Many more are hearing the cry that we must pay more attention to what provides us with all this beauty and bounty.

What can one person do? First, you can focus on becoming the most conscious *you* that is possible. Every act, from the most mundane to the most dramatic, has a ripple effect on everything else. I believe that one of the most significant acts we gardeners can take is to make a commitment to not use chemicals on our lawns and gardens. This simple change, multiplied by millions of gardeners around the world, would have profound effects:

* Decreased amounts of phosphorus runoff into local and regional waterways. This decrease can reduce the algae bloom, which in turn provides a better environment for fish. Over time, it would help return our lakes and streams to swimmable aquatic beauties, like they were only one generation ago.
* More dandelions. Dandelions are par excellence for maintaining liver function, which is considered the seat of health in many cultures. Just by digging up a couple dandelions a week and simmering the roots in water for 20 minutes, then steeping and drinking, you can shift and increase the optimal function of this detoxifying organ.
* Less of your money spent on toxic chemicals. And that in turn decreases the income of corporations that are not investing in the future of our resources but instead are lobbying against

regulations aimed at preventing toxic carcinogens from seeping into our soil, air, and water.

* Increased health of your family and neighbors. Read the warning labels on those chemicals! Better yet, read about the health impact of these chemicals through research published by the World Health Organization or an impartial third party, rather than studies paid for by the chemical companies themselves. After all, the tobacco companies knew their product was cancer-causing long before the public did.

* Keeping pollinators alive and well. They could find plenty of nectar in the wildflowers that go unappreciated in lawns, gardens, and unmown edges. An example is creeping Charlie or ground-ivy (*Glechoma hederacea*). This evergreen perennial begins blooming in spring even before the violets, and provides nectar for the hungry, first-arriving pollinators. (Dandelions are good for pollinators, too!)

* Inspiration for your neighbors to question their own chemical gardening habits. They likely have accepted chemical use as the norm simply because everyone does it. Acting by example is more powerful than trying to convince someone of your beliefs.

Nature has repeatedly shown us that it contains its own medley of superpowers. When we notice, embrace, and utilize Nature's superpowers, we can fulfill what planet Earth intends for us—a safe living environment in which all beings can thrive.

Switching the Paradigm

Another important choice we can make to live in harmony with Earth is to grow our own organic food, and when we need to buy food, to buy organically and locally grown as much as possible. For those who say that organic food is too expensive, I would ask them to consider what the cost is of decreased health—their own and the health of the environment. I know I have lost trust in governments and corporations for looking out for our health. As far as I can see, governments make decisions that protect the profits of chemical companies nearly every time.

I propose that we switch the paradigm. Rather than requiring certified-organic growers to ensure that their crops are protected from pesticide drift, for example, we could require farms that use chemical pesticides to take notes on every day's spraying activity and the steps they have taken to prevent spray drift or contamination of water supplies. And we could ensure that those farms create and maintain buffer zones around their fields to ensure that pollen from their genetically modified crops does not reach the fields of neighboring growers who have pledged to grow non-GMO varieties.

Small-scale organic producers cannot change the direction that our embattled Earth is headed on our own. It is time to reform the cumbersome and difficult regulations that make it difficult for small, eco-friendly producers to thrive, and to place the burden on those who create the toxic substances and follow the damaging agricultural practices that put our natural resources at risk.

I believe that now is the time for breaking down all barriers and separatism. Even something as simple as learning how to relate your thoughts and feelings to your astrological sign breaks down a barrier and puts you into an energetic model with one-twelfth of your fellow humans. I am an Aries, and I am here to start new things and be very enthusiastic about it!

Try this test. When you are fretful and ruminating about your problems, go outside and lie down flat on the Earth. Look at the sky and feel the energy radiating up from beneath your body. Or if you can't lie down, find a spot where you can sit and absorb the beauty of Nature, soak into the oneness. Forget everything mundane, and feel embraced by this love and order of the universe. Go outside at night and look at the stars and galaxies. Become one with them. Consider this a prayer or meditation, to feel one with the spirit. Meditating upon the whole releases your problems. Meditating upon the galaxies is where healing can start, healing for the self and for the planet.

People, plants, planets, and all the other things Nature has provided grab our attention to lift our spirits and guide us on our way. Observe them. Use them. These gifts of Nature inspire me to continue my work and creativity and can do the same for you.

Let's find what unites us in beauty, and cultivate that, like lemon balm sown in Virgo around the Full Moon.

Acknowledgments

I wish to offer thanks to so many who have touched my life as teachers, mentors, friends, and helpers:

Christian Hopka, who asked me to create my first herb garden, planting the seed of herbalism deep in my heart.

The staff at 4E, for keeping the ball rolling while I focused on this project.

Rosemary Gladstar, for contributing the foreword. I reached for the (glad) star, and she responded!

Laurel Redmond, for your friendship, acupuncture, and zillions of discussions on herbs and loving plants.

Matt Wood, for your insightful guidance on the days of the week, planets, and plant associations. And much appreciation for your dedication to herbalism as contributed through your books, teachings, and insights.

William Morris, for opening the window to the connections, cycles, and light that connect us all.

Scott Silverman, my astrology mentor, for being so generous with your time and guidance. And my other astrology teachers, Ryan Evans, Nancy Daniels, and my instructors at Kepler College.

Mark Blumenthal, for being my first friend in the herb world and for championing herbs throughout the world in your dynamic, charismatic, and creative ways.

The other wonderful herb teachers I have had the great fortune to learn from: David Hoffmann, Margi Flint, Isla Burgess, Jill Stansbury, Lisa Ganora, Donnie Yance, and many more. And to the late Maud Grieve and Juliette de Baïracli Levy, the authors of my beloved, worn-out, but not quite used-up books that connected me to many trusted and effective remedies received from the wild and from my garden.

Robin Wall Kimmerer, for the inspiration and love she created with her life's work and *Braiding Sweetgrass*, my current bible.

Robin DiPasquale, your friendship, wisdom, and beauty that inspire me to gently yet profoundly make connections between the natural world and human well-being.

Mary Stankovich, I believe, was moved by Gaia to put me in the Baraboo Bluffs to steward the Earth with David and all the other helpers along the way, providing inspiration and connection to the natural world for thousands at our Open Farm Days throughout the years.

Bob Brackman, thank you for introducing David and me to one another at the Dallas Arboretum, where you looped us together on projects, sparking evident love, written in the stars.

Ley Guimaraes, for your generous and selfless meditation classes for over twenty-five years, especially the rue ritual, which provided a great healing.

Gita Saraydarian and all those at TSG who move Torkom Saraydarian's work into the new ages. His four-volume set *The Wisdom of the Zodiac* provided the inspiration to move forward with connecting people, plants, and planets for increased consciousness on this planet. Your meditations for at least ten years at every Full Moon have polished my various aspects to be a better teacher.

Fern Marshall Bradley and everyone at Chelsea Green Publishing for your guidance and attention to detail to move this dream forward. My excellent editor brother, Tim Hawley, for your time spent with this manuscript, and Laurie Scheer, who got me started on this project.

Faye Jones, Atina Diffley, Harriet Behar, and Linda Halley, for being friends and leaders of the organic movement, paving the way for future generations.

Ann Hawley, my sister and favorite person, who has abundant stories on why I should trust Nature over allopathic concepts.

Jackie Schilz, for your decades of friendship and laughs.

Filipe Barbosa, for your coaching on how to accomplish goals.

Themed Lists for Garden Plants

Tea Garden

American linden (basswood),
   Tilia americana
Anise hyssop, *Agastache foeniculum*
Chamomile, *Matricaria chamomilla*
Lemon balm, *Melissa officinalis*
Lemongrass, *Cymbopogon citratus*
Lemon verbena, *Aloysia citrodora*
Linden, *T. × europaea*
Nettles, *Urtica* spp.
Roses, *Rosa* spp.
Small-leaved linden, *T. cordata*
Spearmint or peppermint,
   Mentha spicata, M. piperita
Tulsi, *Ocimum tenuiflorum*

Fragrant Garden

Artemisias, *Artemisia* spp.
Evergreens, various species
Lavender, *Lavandula angustifolia*
Lemon balm, *Melissa officinalis*
Lemongrass, *Cymbopogon citratus*
Lemon verbena, *Aloysia citrodora*
Rose geranium,
   Pelargonium graveolens
Rosemary, *Rosmarinus officinalis*
Roses, *Rosa* spp. (not all types
   are fragrant)

Sages, *Salvia* spp.
Wisterias, *Wisteria* spp.

Culinary Garden

Basils, *Ocimum* spp.
Cilantro (coriander),
   Coriandrum sativum
Dill, *Anethum graveolens*
Fennel, *Foeniculum vulgare*
Parsley, *Petroselinum crispum*
Rosemary, *Rosmarinus officinalis*
Sage, *Salvia officinalis*
Savory, winter and summer,
   Satureja montana, S. hortensis
Thyme, *Thymus vulgaris*

Medicinal Garden

Black cohosh, *Actaea racemosa*
Calendula, *Calendula officinalis*
Chamomile, *Matricaria chamomilla*
Echinacea, *Echinacea purpurea*
Lavender, *Lavandula angustifolia*
Lemon balm, *Melissa officinalis*
Mints, *Mentha* spp.
Roses, *Rosa* spp.
Sage, *Salvia officinalis*
Skullcap, *Scutellaria lateriflora*
St. John's wort, *Hypericum perforatum*

Thyme, *Thymus vulgaris*
Witch hazel, *Hamamelis virginiana*
Yarrow, *Achillea millefolium*

Biblical or Meditation Garden

Angelica (common),
    Angelica archangelica
Calendula, *Calendula officinalis*
Damask rose, *Rosa damascena*
Hyssop, *Hyssopus officinalis*
Lady's mantle, *Alchemilla vulgaris*
Rosemary, *Rosmarinus officinalis*
Rue, *Ruta graveolens*
Sage, *Salvia officinalis*
Tulsi, *Ocimum tenuiflorum*

Butterfly Garden

Bee balm, *Monarda* spp.
Bergamot, *Citrus bergamia*
Catnip, *Nepeta cataria*
Chives, *Allium schoenoprasum*
Echinacea, *Echinacea* spp.
Garlic chives, *Allium tuberosum*
Lavender, *Lavandula angustifolia*
Milkweeds, *Asclepias* spp.
Mints, *Mentha* spp.
Oreganos, *Origanum* spp.
Parsley, *Petroselinum crispum*

Sages, *Salvia* spp.
Tulsi, *Ocimum tenuiflorum*

Four Directions or Humors Garden

East, First Quarter,
spring, sanguine, Air signs
Lobelia, *Lobelia inflata*
Marshmallow, *Althaea officinalis*
Solomon's seal,
    Polygonatum multiflorum

South, Full Moon,
summer, choleric, Fire signs
Milk thistle, *Silybum marianum*
Rosemary, *Rosmarinus officinalis*
Wormwood, *Artemisia absinthium*

West, Last Quarter,
autumn, melancholy, Fire signs
Broadleaf plantain, *Plantago major*
Echinacea, *Echinacea* spp.
Lady's mantle, *Alchemilla vulgaris*

North, New Moon,
winter, phlegmatic, Water signs
Hyssop, *Hyssopus officinalis*
Thyme, *Thymus vulgaris*
Winter savory, *Satureja montana*

Themed Lists for Decorative Wreaths

A Wreath to Celebrate a Birth

Agrimony for thankfulness
Calla for magnificent beauty
Cedar for strength
China rose for beauty always new
Chrysanthemum for cheerfulness
    under adversity
Cinquefoil for maternal affection
Coreopsis for always cheerful
Cowslip for "you are my divinity"
Crocus for youthful gladness
Currants for "you please all"
Dittany of Crete for birth
Hawthorn for hope
Hyacinth for sport, games, and play
Lucerne (alfalfa) for life
Magnolia for love of nature
Marjoram for blushing
Mint for virtue
Moss for maternal love
Mugwort for happiness
    and tranquility
Myrtle for love
Periwinkle for pleasures of memory
Poplar for courage
Rose for love
Rosemary for remembrance

Sage for domestic virtue
Thyme for activity

A Wreath for a Graduation or Other Life Landmark

Angelica for inspiration
Bay for glory
Black poplar for courage
Cabbage for profit
Canary grass for perseverance
Canterbury bells for
    acknowledgment
Cherry tree for good education
Chicory for frugality
Chrysanthemum for cheerfulness
    under adversity
Cloves for dignity
Corn for riches
Elm for dignity
Fennel for worthy of all praise
Gladiolus for strength of character
Red clover for industry
Scarlet geranium for comforting
Thyme for activity

A Wreath for a Funeral

Amaranth for immortality
Arborvitae for unchanging friendship

Azalea for "true to the end"

Bay for glory

Elm for dignity

Geranium (a dark-flowered variety)
  for melancholy

Ivy for fidelity, friendship,
  and marriage

Mint for virtue

Mullein for good nature

Pear for comfort

Rose for love

Rosemary for remembrance

Sage for esteem

Thyme for activity

Wormwood for absence

Yew for sorrow

Zinnia for thoughts of
  absent friends

Resources

Seed and Gardening Supply Companies

A.M. Leonard Horticultural Tool and Supply
www.amleo.com

Fedco Seeds
www.fedcoseeds.com

Gardener's Supply Company
www.gardeners.com

Johnny's Selected Seeds
www.johnnyseeds.com

Richters Herbs
www.richters.com

Strictly Medicinal Seeds
https://strictlymedicinalseeds.com

Astrology Schools and Teachers

Academy for Astrological Medicine
www.academyforastrological
medicine.com

Forrest Center for Evolutionary Astrology
https://forrestastrology.center

Kepler College
https://keplerclasses.org

William Morris
Astrology, herbalism, and acutonics
https://acutonics.com/instructors
/bio/william-r.-morris-phd-daom-lac

Herbalism Schools and Teachers

California School of Herbal Studies
https://cshs.com

Chestnut School of Herbal Medicine
https://chestnutherbs.com

Colorado School of Clinical Herbalism
https://clinicalherbalism.com

Matthew Wood Institute of Herbalism
www.matthewwoodinstituteof
herbalism.com

Northeast School of Botanical Medicine
https://7song.com

Rosemary Gladstar's Science and Art of Herbalism
https://scienceandartofherbalism
.com

The School of Evolutionary Herbalism
www.evolutionaryherbalism.com

Vermont Center for
Integrative Herbalism
https://vtherbcenter.org

Wildwood Institute
https://wildwoodinstitute.com

Organic Growing

Canadian Organic Growers
https://cog.ca

Marbleseed
https://marbleseed.org

Northeast Organic
Farming Association
https://nofa.org

Oregon Tilth
https://tilth.org

Organic Growers School
www.organicgrowersschool.org

Rodale Institute
https://rodaleinstitute.org

USDA National Organic Program
www.usda.gov/topics/organic

Herbal Product Companies

Check your local farmers market to find your local herbalist and herb formulator!

Avena Botanicals
www.avenabotanicals.com

Four Elements Organic Herbals
https://fourelementsherbals.com

Herbs, Etc.
https://herbsetc.com

Mountain Rose Herbs
https://mountainroseherbs.com

Oshala Farm
https://oshalafarm.com

Selected Bibliography

Bailey, Alice A. *Esoteric Astrology, Vol. 2: A Treatise on the Seven Rays*. New York: Lucis Publishing, 1971.

Boland, Yasmin. *Moonology: Working with the Magic of Lunar Cycles*. Carlsbad, CA: Hay House, 2016.

Buhner, Stephen Harrod. *The Lost Language of Plants: The Ecological Importance of Plant Medicines to Life on Earth*. White River Junction, VT: Chelsea Green Publishing, 2002.

Burk, Kevin. *Astrology: Understanding the Birth Chart: A Comprehensive Guide to Classical Interpretation*. Woodbury, MN: Llewellyn Publications, 2003.

De Carvalho, Helena Avelar, and Luis Campos Ribeiro. *On the Heavenly Spheres: A Treatise on Traditional Astrology*. Tempe, AZ: American Federation of Astrologers, 2010.

Forrest, Steven. *The Book of the Moon: Discovering Astrology's Lost Dimension*. Borrego Springs, CA: Seven Paws Press, 2013.

Ganora, Lisa. *Herbal Constituents: Foundations of Phytochemistry: A Holistic Approach for Students and Practitioners of Botanical Medicine*. Louisville, CO: HerbalChem Press, 2009.

Gehl, Jennifer T., and Marc S. Micozzi. *The Science of Planetary Signatures in Medicine: Restoring the Cosmic Foundations of Healing*. Rochester, VT: Healing Arts Press, 2017.

Gillett, Roy. *The Secret Language of Astrology: The Illustrated Key to Unlocking the Secrets of the Stars*. London: Watkins, 2011.

Green, James. *The Herbal Medicine-Makers' Handbook: A Home Manual*. Freedom, CA: The Crossing Press, 2000.

Hand, Robert. *Horoscope Symbols*. Richmond, VA: Bushwood Books, 1981.

Harris, John, and Jim Rickards. *Moon Gardening: Ancient and Natural Ways to Grow Healthier, Tastier Food*. London: John Blake, 2016.

Hill, Judith A. *Medical Astrology: A Guide to Planetary Pathology*. Portland, OR: Stellium Press, 2005.

Junius, Manfred M. *The Practical Handbook of Plant Alchemy: An Herbalist's Guide to Preparing Medicinal Essences, Tinctures, and Elixirs*. Rochester, VT: Healing Arts Press, 1993.

Klocek, Dennis. *Seeking Spirit Vision: Essays on Developing Imagination*. Fair Oaks, CA: Rudolf Steiner College Press, 2001.

Kranich, Ernst Michael. *Planetary Influences upon Plants: A Cosmological Botany*. Translated by Ulla Chadwick and Austin Chadwick. Wyoming, RI: Bio-Dynamic Literature, 1984.

Lewi, Grant. *Astrology for the Millions*. Woodbury, MN: Llewellyn Publications, 2002.

Lewi, Grant. *Heaven Knows What*. Woodbury, MN: Llewellyn Publications, 2022.

Llewellyn Publishing. *Llewellyn's 2023 Moon Sign Book: Plan Your Life by the Cycles of the Moon*. Woodbury, MN: Llewellyn Publications, 2022.

Morris, William. *Cycles in Medical Astrology: Revolutionary Tools for the Practitioner*. Vancouver: 33 publishing, 2018.

Obert, Charles, and Nina Gryphon. *The Classical Seven Planets: Source Texts and Meaning*. Minneapolis: Almuten Press, 2020.

Obert, Charles. *Introduction to Traditional Natal Astrology: A Complete Working Guide for Modern Astrologers*. Minneapolis: Almuten Press, 2015.

Pyle, Jack R., and Taylor Reese. *Raising with the Moon: The Complete Guide to Gardening and Living by the Signs of the Moon*. Boone, NC: Parkway Publishers, 2004.

Riotte, Louise. *Astrological Gardening: The Ancient Wisdom of Successful Planting and Harvesting by the Stars*. New York: Wings Books, 1995.

Rudhyar, Dane. *The Galactic Dimension of Astrology: The Sun Is Also a Star*. New York: Dutton, 1975.

Saraydarian, Torkom. *The Wisdom of the Zodiac, 2nd ed. Vol. 1–4*. Cave Creek, AZ: TSG Publishing Foundation, 2013.

Saraydarian, Torkom. *Symphony of the Zodiac*. Scottsdale, AZ: Saraydarian Institute, 1988.

Thomas, Robert B. *The Old Farmer's Almanac: Calculated on a New and Improved Plan for the Year of Our Lord 2023*. Dublin, NH: Yankee Publishing Incorporated, 2022.

Thun, Maria. *The Biodynamic Year: Increasing Yield, Quality and Flavour: 100 Helpful Tips for the Gardener or Smallholder*. Translated by Matthew Barton. Forest Row, UK: Temple Lodge, 2010.

Thun, Titia, and Friedrich Thun. *The North American Maria Thun Biodynamic Almanac 2023*. Edinburgh: Floris Books, 2022.

Waldin, Monty. *Biodynamic Gardening: Grow Healthy Plants and Amazing Produce with the Help of the Moon and Nature's Cycles*. New York: DK Publishing, 2015.

Wood, Matthew. *The Practice of Traditional Western Herbalism: Basic Doctrine, Energetics, and Classification*. Berkeley, CA: North Atlantic Books, 2004.

Index

Note: Page numbers in *italics* refer to photographs and figures. Page numbers followed by *t* refer to tables.

Index

About the Author

Savanna Rose Stevens

Jane Hawley Stevens plants, harvests, and creates herbal wellness for her Four Elements Organic Herbals brand (www.fourelementsherbals.com) from her 130-acre farm in Wisconsin. She is a knowledgeable elder in the Midwest herbalism community and an established figure in the herbal products industry. She and her husband, David Stevens, have been at the forefront of organics, becoming certified-organic growers in 1990. Jane and David received the Outstanding Organic Farmer of the Year award in 2020 from MOSES (now Marbleseed), an organization that works to grow the organic-farming movement in the Midwest. Jane has been designing herb gardens and growing herbs for more than forty years, and she is also well-known as a speaker and teacher, offering courses and workshops through her apothecary and farm, as well as at health food stores and conferences. She spends her time gardening, hiking, biking, and skiing to be surrounded by the beauty and awe that can be experienced only outdoors. You can find her at night, gazing at the stars and planets with reverence for the opportunity to be an advocate for Nature and all its wonderment.